Midnight Peaches, Two O'Clock Patience

A COLLECTION OF ESSAYS, POEMS, AND SHORT STORIES
ON WOMANHOOD AND THE SPIRIT

Janet Stickmon

BROKEN SHACKLE PUBLISHING • Oakland

BROKEN SHACKLE PUBLISHING
P.O. Box 20312
Oakland, CA 94620
www.brokenshackle.wordpress.com
brokenshacklepublishing@gmail.com

Library of Congress Control Number: 2012913351
ISBN 978-0-9759908-2-7

The broken shackle logo is a trademark of Broken Shackle Publishing
owned by Janet Stickmon.
Front & Back Cover Photograph: © 2011 Janet Stickmon
Cover Design: © 2012 Design Action Collective

to all those
who make flowers bloom
&
to all flowers
who want to bloom

CONTENTS

Yahaira is a devout Catholic who once knew truth, and is now attempting to find it again.   She knows her honesty and sensitivity are her greatest attributes but feels that somehow these qualities aren't enough.

Her truths are told in "Yahaira's Love" and "are you real."

Dr. Gold Taraji is an African-American woman who just turned 40. Taraji has been a physics professor for 10 years and recently gave birth to a baby girl. She enters a new phase in her life as a single mom and well-recognized community healer. She looks forward to forming new relationships in light of her latest wave of self-love. "Wait for Me," "Breastmilk," "Hell's Body," "Spirit," "Birthmark," "Sexy," "Here's the Truth," "Leave Tomorrow," and "Love Musings" are her revelations.

I am a wife, mother, and teacher. I am Blackapina. I savor Life.

Together, my sisters and I share our stories.

Exhaustion of Beauty

I became entangled with places I vowed never to revisit.

Too many doubles existed within my head without my
knowing.

I am split in two daily
Into
Days leaving the dawn to meet the evening.
And I am left at once…bereft.

Right past my present I walk into my former self
          Searching.
I begin again
          Walking toward my present.
I sink beneath myself where the scent of candle wax meets
urn,
Turn around to a time when I would struggle to define and
Refine myself,
          Only to find myself lost:

A recluse crawls with outstretched hand and raw knees
Through white and bleached inconsistencies
A memory imbibed with the stench of pulsing membranes
and callous bodies

Gray circles beneath her eyes testify before fellow hearts that
tried too hard
Vestiges of collapsed desire.

Listen and listen, for her body is a crucible for rage, and love,
vision and fear
And love, bitter, and ache and
        Sweetness
Melting in the heat,
        Misinformed conscience waiting for the proper
moment
To revive herself.
But don't tell her this is where hope resides.
        Because she may discover her strength.
For she may rise with a rage
        Frightening venom into a stupor.

Claiming her space
        With one step,
Causing a room to expand.

She, yes she, no she, will show them goodness.
Misery no longer.

Beauty emerges sending clouds into confusion
        Wondering why she didn't rise sooner.

Yajaira's Love

I always look forward to meeting Larkin, Yajaira thought to herself as she drove to his office. She stops at an intersection and reminisces:

I remember when we sat in my car, enjoying the view of the East Bay from the top of the Oakland hills. We talked for hours as we waited for sunset. If I had something to say that I couldn't quite articulate, he waited patiently. He always waits. His complete attention anticipates a beauty in what I have yet to express. His patience coaxes the words from me with ease. I can't help but be completely transparent before him. Because I have his patience, I have no need to hide anything; my faults are not made beautiful; instead, they are left alone—accepted and held. I am not beautiful because of what his eyes see; I am beautiful because his eyes allow me to be. His vision dares not dictate the form my beauty takes. This beauty defies the curves and shades of his imagination. He knows that it is boundless and beyond his comprehension. So he cannot help but bow before it and let that beauty breathe. I never thought a man's patience could be so arousing. Now I know nothing sexier than this virtue.

◊

She finally arrives. She knocks and peeks around the side of the door. Sitting behind his desk, Larkin motions her in as he finishes a phone call. Yajaira walks into his office and sits across from him, looking at the bookshelf as she waits.

"Uh, huh, uh huh, I know exactly what you mean,"

he says, half-interested in the phone conversation.

Every few seconds, he steals quick glances of Yajaira. She is wearing a lavender turtleneck and jeans, sitting with her legs crossed. At second glance, he sees her pull her sepia braids over one shoulder as she bends down to see a book low on the shelf. She turns his way, and he quickly averts his gaze, looking as if he'd been honing in on some random spot on his desk. The snapshots he took with his eyes made him curious enough to stare, but wise enough not to.

With the phone still in his hand, he walks to the shelf, remembering a book that might interest Yajaira. He leans over her, searching the shelves for Audre Lorde's *Sister Outsider*. She's not sure if this is deliberate, but she feels the warmth of his body close to hers and it makes her uncomfortable, yet excited. Sitting perfectly still, she waits, wondering how much longer it will take.

Larkin is stalling. He smells gardenias and cocoa butter. The scent rises off Yajaira's dark honey skin. He stops to breathe her in. Larkin doesn't want to move, but he also fears arousing her suspicion. When Larkin finds the book, he slowly hands it to her with a seductive look of invitation, and within the same instant quickly snatches back his provocative energy. Covering the receiver, he whispers, "I think you'll like this."

"Thank you," she says, smiling. As she peeks at the book, Larkin takes a step back, brushing back his long bangs with his fingers, lightly biting his bottom lip searching for a way to prevent his hormone buzz from becoming obvious.

Is he flirting? she wonders. She quickly dismisses the idea, forcing herself to believe she imagined it. However, the more she resists the thought, the more she hopes it's more than her imagination. She doubts she should be feeling this way, especially toward a priest.

9/15/00

Dear Larkin,

How are you? I know you're workin' hard. As for me, I'm doing well. Trying to take a break from everything. Just returned from a jog around the lake. The leaves are so beautiful today. I hope you're enjoying them. If not, get outta that office, and stomp on some leaves or somethin'! I love fall. I never knew leaves changed into so many different colors until I moved out here.

Anyways, um, I've been wanting to tell you something for awhile. Never quite sure how. I was too embarrassed to tell you in person. I felt like I had to tell you soon.

Please accept this poem. Hope it makes sense. Here it goes....

are you real

i believe in people

people teach me many things

and people prove me wrong daily

no

                         what I want to tell you is....

if i could touch your lips

i'd say, *don't speak*

if i could hold your pen

i'd say, *don't write*

let's stop writing

let's stop talking

i want to see you

see you strut with certain pride and quiet step

see you wink the way you did in June

let our eyes meet the way they did in July

your heart probe my thoughts like in August

let our arms touch the way they did at the start of fall

let our laughter become entangled in the absurdity of it all

the poor timing of it all

the magic of it all

and laugh at the people who don't understand

what's between us

so, what is between us?

i don't know

too beautiful to name

but i like it

how it came unannounced

healed us without notice

it was simple

it was fun

and

i miss you

but it might be temporary

                                      fleeting

◊

is it okay to meet again?

can we listen to each other's voices

let us meet again

i want nothing from you

but your presence

when you are present

i grow

◊

i miss you

i hope it will be the same

but maybe it was meant to be temporary

                                        fleeting

◊

here we are

your arm is too close to mine

and too many eyes are watching

too many eyes

i watch you stretch your arms

your sea turtle stretches with you

swimming toward your fingertips

i want to stroke your tattoo

any chance to touch you

study its lines, its jagged edges, its spirals

study your skin

it must be soft and gentle

like the way you say my name

oops

but too many eyes

too many eyes asking questions

who cares

may i hold you

the way I wanted to hold you years ago

before we met

when i thought you didn't exist

when our feet touched the same soil

paths never crossed

i wasn't ready for you

you weren't ready for me

are we ready now

◊

are you sure

    you're real?

because i trust people

and i die daily to false hope

because people disappoint me

but i still believe in people

so tell me are you real

please tell me

        don't hurt me

tell me

please show me

        you are real

        With Love,

        Yahaira

Being Pregnant

I absolutely loved being pregnant! Being pregnant was the greatest privilege I had ever experienced. Never had I felt so beautiful and so well-respected in my entire life. To be more than just a vessel for human life...to be a cocreator with the Divine—the God I'd known through many years of love, doubt, disbelief, and faith. The God who's known me through prayer and meditation. It was only after my pregnancy that I realized I'd become closer to God. I suppose it's no wonder I felt so beautiful and so alive and so clear: I was in union with the Divine.

If humanity is created in the image and likeness of God like Genesis 1: 26-27 says, and if according to the Yoruba, the *Emi* is the divine element of a person that links a person to God, and if the Bantu-Kongo believe that a human being is both container and instrument of Divine energy, then I caught a glimpse of what it means to be in union with the Divine.[1]

And in my limited knowledge as a human being, I felt this was true only because everything in the world seemed to both make sense and be a complete mystery at the same time. And I was okay with that.

I remember wanting to protect this unborn child from the hands (or the presence) of anyone with foul energy. This is why I rarely let anyone other than my husband touch my belly. At the same time, I wanted to be careful not to

---

[1] Wade Nobles, *Seeking the Sakhu: Foundational Writings for an African Psychology* (Chicago: Third World Press, 2006), 332-335.

protect her too much. Before I was pregnant, my husband told me about a woman who thought of her unborn child as a generator. I liked this image and wanted to think of my baby in a similar fashion—this unborn child generating energy, energy that I could harness if I needed to ward off evil. I was also considering the Akan and Christian belief that an unborn child is intimately connected to the Divine prior to entering this existence. As such, she would have greater access to wisdom that I do not have.

When a woman is pregnant, it is common for people to understand that she is carrying around another human being. This goes without saying. However, I was puzzled by how there was such little discussion about a woman's body housing two spirits—her own and her child's. I was curious about the sort of intermingling that takes place between the spirits throughout the duration of a woman's pregnancy. I certainly noticed a difference within me that could only be partially explained by the hormonal changes.

I never experienced so much clarity, vibrancy, and intolerance for bullshit in my life. The combination of our two spirits seemed unbeatable. Regardless of whether I was at home, at work, or at the grocery store, I remember thinking, *If someone wants to mess with me, bring it! There are two of us now!* It's funny...today, when I look at my daughter, seeing how courageous she is, seeing how strong-willed and persuasive she is...how fierce she is...I now understand where my will to fight came from.

The Bionic Nose

Because I am into the full sensory experience, I love to see, touch, smell, and hear the fine details that shape Creation. If I don't practice noticing the world around me with all my senses, I feel like I don't have a clear sense of reality and will consequently miss out on what life has to offer. Taking in different scents, like the sweet smells of candles and flowers, has always brought me great pleasure. Throughout my life, I've learned that I tend to associate a scent with profound or traumatic experiences. I discovered that the faintest smell can trigger vivid memories: the aroma of sweet rice boiling in coconut milk reminds me of Momma's bright smile; the scent of Tide brings me back to being 13 when our house burned down and how hard my parents tried to wash out the stench of smoke from our clothes; the brisk trace of salt in moist air reminds me of every trip to the beach and how much peace I find there.

I thought I was fairly tuned into the outside world until I became pregnant. Pregnancy granted me a heightened sense of smell. Early in my first trimester, I was driving around Oakland and pulled into a shopping center on 51st Street and Broadway. Found a parking space next to Boston Market and stepped out of the car. Immediately, I was bombarded by at least 40 different scents: Wendy's french fries across the street; roasted chicken behind me at Boston Market; Starbucks coffee on the other end of the parking lot; car exhaust from cars speeding down Broadway; gutter water flowing along the curb and a multitude of other smells I had no names for. Still holding onto the car door with one foot on the pavement, time stopped for an instant:

> *I was the new lead in Mission Impossible*
> *and with my cyborg contacts, not only was I scanning the faces*
> *around me,*
> *I was scanning every odor in that damn parking lot,*
> *calculating how many milliseconds remained before I'd vomit from*
> *this olfactory assault.*

I don't remember how much time I had left, but it wasn't much. Right away, I closed the door and just sat there, looking out the windshield, wondering what just happened.

If we could imagine the infinite number of aromas and odors that exist in the world—the pungent and foul, the pleasant and enticing—and paint each one a different color, we'd see millions of waves of various frequencies and amplitudes floating in the air, colliding into each other, overlapping to the point where no single scent could be recognized. That day in the parking lot, I smelled all the scents in the world and stopped yearning for that clear sense of reality I always search for. I had enough clarity for one day.

As much as I wanted to impress my friends with my bionic sense of smell and show off how many different scents I could identify in a room, this new ability didn't always feel like a gift; at times, it was rather isolating and felt like a curse. Since I had such an acute sense of smell, I found myself constantly being accused of smelling "phantom smells," as if anything I smelled was just my imagination.

I remember smelling gas in the kitchen one day. I called up PG&E and reported a gas leak. Someone came out to check the house and found nothing. He detected no odor, and yet I still felt nauseous from a distinct gas smell that was definitely there.

"Superpowers don't exist if nobody believes you," I sobbed as he drove away. It occurred to me that any powers, any gifts people profess to have require validation by at least one other person before they're considered "real"—and even then, it all depends on whether or not the world deems that person credible. So many experiences of pregnant women are dismissed as a distortion of reality. And still we yell, "This is real because I say it's real and because the pregnant women behind me and in front of me say it's real; all pregnant women before me and after me will tell you what's real. We're not crazy. We're not exaggerating." And yet, no one hears us. Rarely do we consider that maybe the rat race of tangled routines that govern our days and nights might be numbing us to reality. If we really knew how much richness *and* toxicity were embedded in all that we smell, eat, and hear, we would collapse in astonishment.

I smelled gas, and I knew it!   The following day, I called PG&E a second time.   Once again, someone came out but this time did a more thorough investigation. Sure enough, there was a gas leak; it was beneath the house and was traced to an old broken floor heater in the livingroom. The gas seeped into the house and was most concentrated in the kitchen. He immediately shut off the gas line leading to the heater and told us exactly what needed to be repaired.

This superpower was no curse. I knew what was real long before it was confirmed by an outside source. My antenna to the world was finely tuned for the safety of my unborn child. Thank God for this divine design—my bionic nose saved my family.

Wait for Me

four months to go
and I hear you call me
for the first time
while praying

i wake

you trust
i am strong
you trust I have some insight
you lost touch with
you trust me since I know Nyame's voice

you want to protect me
but draw from my energy—my spirit like a generator
my spirit—a water well

you wait
not wanting me to
lose my innocence
my purity
not wanting to
expose me to the stress
the evil
you see everyday

i hear you apologize for asking
for my help

i wish I had a voice to tell you
there's no need to say sorry

before I was a thought
i heard them when they accused you
of religious malpractice
of brainwashing
of being disturbing
imbalanced
devious

and when you fought back
they said you attacked them

                the innocent

they called you judgmental

and still
all the while
seeking
to win your favor
and be your friend

                to absolve them

of guilt

volatile reactions to
good
warrant no pity

they only confirm
justice is yours

and then I heard you question
what sort of world
you were bringing me into
when Bhutto was assassinated
when your neighbors were killed
when teachers call you
crying
asking
why they were fired
for saving lives

when adults twice your age
wept in your arms
i heard you ask
how someone with decades of life experience
could curl up
motionless
stifled by self-doubt
before fragile pre-pubescent egos
with big mouths
shifty eyes
and shaky legs

should fear be this powerful?

these deaths made you hungry

                                    and so I too became

hungry

i kick

kick you hard

i kick when you speak of what you hate
i kick because I hate how you're treated

then you eat

and I sleep when you pat my feet
and play Ray Brown
i kick now
because I am full

i punch because
i love what you love
i punch you hard
because this world is too much
and yet it's just enough
i punch because I don't understand
what you don't understand

but when you pat my feet
and bounce on the yoga ball
i sleep

understand
you don't just carry a second body
within you

i am Second Spirit

so I will kick and punch with you
together we are stronger

three months to go
and you call me your little conscience
you say I give you clarity
i say you inspire me

i watched you stare
arrogance in the face
wound it with words
for all to see

you were in control
and yet you were shook
this ugly scene shook me
so I kicked
punched

grandpa
momma
auntie
boss
wife
mistress
mailman
all enamored with his polished appearance
manufactured charm

confusing

his arrogance for confidence
his bold assertions for wisdom
never noticing
his claims go unsupported
satisfied with the sound of his voice   intelligence(?)

and so they fear him
and stay silent

i tell you
the pompous are fragile
it takes only a few featherweight blows
to the head to deflate a self-absorbed Messiah complex

he once proclaimed he meant no harm
but when no one believed him
his eyes became rotten with rage
and you saw his insides harden

is this how evil moves?

i say
evil engages in cottonball warfare

making all that leaks from orifice Divine
sound innocuous
though noxious
in truth and nature

it insults   and believes it's

kind
pompous   yet appears
selfless
skilled at playing victim   after inciting a
war

so entangled in its delusions
it eventually destroys itself
overwhelmed by its greed
always wanting more
dissatisfied with triumph
wants desperately to feel again
like a cutter
one final test of power
control
to inflict pain upon itself

evil is tied to pain
when a wound is torn open
evil lashes out
and bares its weakness for all to witness

momma
when you discover this link
evil is not so clever
not so handsome
not so daunting
all it takes is one courageous cottonball
to shatter big mouths with shaky legs
and evil will devour itself

three more weeks...
you are calm
relaxed
smiling
holding cottonballs

you are clear
house is clean
but not too sterile
you protect me
but don't shelter me

in the beginning you said

> *If I could spare you my flaws and failings,*
> *I would.*
> *If I could protect you from the*
> *emotional sickness of the Living,*
> *I would.*

but since you can't
train me to
maneuver in it
fight
and heal

train me for
physical
emotional

combat

please momma
along with
diapers
toys
wet wipes
calendula
don't forget to pack
boxing gloves
kali sticks
knives
ace bandages
arnica

so I can hold Tigger in one hand
and a kali stick in the other
wear diapers and onesies by day
and face mask and cape by night

don't forget to pack a pen
journal
dictionary

when I come
i will only have the motor skills to scratch my face
kick off my socks

but soon
i'll use all

you've given me
to navigate this world
the world you have so many questions about

wait for me Momma
i'm on my way

Teacher-Mom

On paper and voicemails, I identify as a professor. At conferences—a professor. In the classroom—a professor. I've found that **identifying as such is so important for us as people of color who have students who've never had a professor of color before**. It becomes important to recognize our title while at the same time not turn it into such a big deal that it alienates us from our students. This is tricky.

In everyday speech, I speak of myself as a teacher. Teaching is one of the most selfless, prophetic professions one could ever undertake. I put it up there with the nurse, the doctor, the therapist, the minister, the *curandera*, the *babaylan*, the griot, and other healers like custodians, crossing guards, and tow truck drivers. Any qualities I claim to embody as a professor is because of the people I have emulated. Teachers, priests, nuns, indigenous healers, counselors, homeless women and men, the anonymous passenger on a plane, friends, family, and other loved ones have all had a hand in my development as a human being and consequently as a teacher. If I am ever complimented on my teaching, I have no choice but to remember that I am a direct reflection of the loving people I have come in contact with throughout my life. When my mentors come out to support me, I learn, surprisingly, that my success is their triumph. My beauty is their splendor. My happiness, their rapture.

Teachers have the potential to be healers. Not saviors. Not omnipotent leaders...but humble healers who know that any liberatory catharsis experienced by our students (as a result of our teaching) occurs because we are instruments of a greater power. We are humble healers who must also be open to learning from our students. The gifts we share are bestowed upon us by the Divine. This is a tremendous responsibility, and one must not intellectualize it too much otherwise one might miss the beauty of it, the mystery of it and collapse from the enormity of it.

There are things that I do in the classroom that I cannot take credit for. Like the perfect thought that comes at the perfect moment: and there I am, left surprised by my own words. The positive impact we have on others—even on the days we don't feel good about ourselves—fascinates me. Such things can only be explained by the Divine. It is vital to call upon the universe, Goddess/God, goddesses/gods, and the ancestors to reconcile the interstices that bind our greatest expectations to our greatest disappointments; that bind our greatest lack of understanding to our greatest revelations.

*

When my daughter was born, this identity as teacher/professor was tested. I was with her for five months before I returned to work. And when I stepped foot into the classroom, I didn't feel like a professor or a teacher. I felt like I had never taught before. I was lost in my own classroom. I stumbled over my words. My old lesson plans seemed outdated, and I felt clumsy trying to teach from them. I was painfully ashamed and considered ending my career as a teacher. I couldn't figure out what happened to me. I thought that it had something to do with using baby talk for five months straight. But I felt it was much more than that.

In the past when I've been in these awkward, painful transitional phases, I knew this signaled a new exciting beginning. So I waited and rode the wave. Eventually, it occurred to me that I couldn't possibly expect myself to be the same person, the same teacher, after bringing a life into the world. I had changed permanently, and what was painful for me in that moment, I imagine ran parallel to the trauma my daughter felt when she was born. Perhaps, Goddess is in the transition phase right now, preparing to give birth to a new me. And I just need to get out of the way to let that birth happen.

Breastmilk

I romanticized breastfeeding. I thought as soon as I breastfed my baby, I would instantly feel an overwhelming rush of affection for her deep within my bosom; I imagined being completely content, holding her in my arms day and night. I thought we would share some unspoken understanding that I was hers and she was mine and this would remain forever—even beyond the grave.

A host of stories told by other mothers, as well as loads of workshops and literature discussing the joys and benefits of breastfeeding all fed these beliefs. I believed these things even on the day she was born when the doctors raised her up to me and placed her on my breast. Immediately, she began to nurse and I wept uncontrollably. It wasn't the mere sight of her that caused my tears to fall. Truth be told, the instant Baby left my womb and entered the open air, her face didn't immediately tug at my heart. It didn't completely register that she was the reason I'd been pushing. Instead, I was more relieved that the cold chills, the trembling, the teeth chattering, the waves of pain radiating throughout my body (feeling like the worst case of dysentery known to humankind) had all come to an end. I was so happy that all of this was over that I forgot why I was pushing so hard. When they raised Baby toward me, I thought, *Oh yeah, a baby!* Then, my first experience of breastfeeding came and Baby began suckling. She knew exactly what she was doing—at less than a minute old. What a mystery to me! I crossed the waterfall of my tears and entered her world.

During the first three days, colostrum came from my

breasts; some said it would be thick and yellow, but for me it was a clear and slightly thin gel. It was rich with proteins and antibodies good for Baby's immune system. At this time, I wasn't exactly sure if she was latching on properly. I was also worried that my breastmilk would not come. I didn't have any real basis for this. I had a tendency to imagine the worst case scenario so I could be "emotionally equipped" to deal with disappointment. In other words, I have often prepared to be disappointed. It's a worn-out coping mechanism that served its purpose for a time and proved itself quite useful. However, it was not necessary now, nor was it healthy for a new mother. I thought that if something were to go wrong, it would happen to me, though I had no evidence of anything "going wrong" throughout the pregnancy or even during labor.

Perhaps my breasts wouldn't yield milk because these were the same breasts that came out lopsided in the seventh grade. First the left, then later the right. And even when they did become the same size, it wasn't as though a bra was all that necessary. There wasn't too much to hold up, push up, or show off. It was just like, *Okay, I guess I better wear a bra just in case I get hit during kickball or volleyball or something.*

I worried and waited. The second day came. No milk. The third day came. No milk. My worries were becoming a reality. I called Kaiser, scheduled a phone appointment, and spoke with Dr. Deeptah Dubashi. She said that my milk might still come in but if not, relying on a bottle instead of breastmilk would be just fine. After all, she had to eat.

"She'll still grow up healthy and strong. I was a bottle-fed baby, and I think I turned out pretty well." She and I laughed for a quick moment while I held in my real question, *But would she ever bond with me?*

No matter how much reassurance Dr. Dubashi gave me, I wasn't satisfied. Giving my baby formula was not how I imagined caring for my child.

Sterling, Baby, and I went to Longs Drugs (my all-time favorite store) to look for baby bottles and formula. I sat with Baby in the back seat while Sterling drove. I could tell he was worried about me. He caught me staring out the window. "How are you?" he asked.

I was awful.   Lifeless, sleep-deprived, and disappointed.   I was convinced that after three days of parenting, I was a horrible parent.   What kind of mother can't breastfeed her own child?! I was beating myself up for something I couldn't control. And at the same time, I had to accept the fact that my child had to eat, and if she needed formula because Momma's breastmilk didn't come in, then so be it.

While Sterling waited in the car with Baby, I walked alone to the infant section of Longs. I walked in totally unprepared, having done no research, hoping the labels on the packaging would give me clues about what was best for my baby. There were too many choices, and I cried as I examined the labels of bottles, nipples, and formula, surprised by how many brands and shapes and sizes and colors these things came in. I didn't bother researching any of this while I was pregnant because I was planning on breastfeeding. But there I was, overwhelmed and confused.   I finally made a decision, bought what I needed, and left.

ɟ

Sterling gave Baby and I some privacy as I tried to feed her. Feeling nervous and somewhat useless, he poked his head in to ask, "Is she eating?" Then, two and five minutes later, again he popped in, "Is she eating?"

As I brought the bottle close to her, she took a taste and then immediately wrapped her little forearms around my wrist and pulled the bottle into her mouth. The child was strong. And apparently hungry. "She's eating, she's eating," I yelled. She had about an ounce to two ounces of formula. I was happy, and yet still disappointed.

Our doula came later that night, the end of the third day, and showed me how to express milk from my breasts. It didn't work, and this first-time Mom was anxious and sweaty. The doula gave it a try and expressed two large drops of breastmilk and said, "See, it's here." I cried the same tears I wept when Baby nursed for the first time in the delivery room. My breastmilk actually came.

ɟ

The first two weeks of breastfeeding was lonesome. Offering Baby shelter from distraction, I brought her into the master bedroom, dreading my routine retreat back into the silence of this space. Alone in that room was me, Baby, and the damn timer—the one that timed me (like a judgmental mother-in-law) to make sure Baby was fed about 7-13 minutes on each breast.   I felt like I was being used.   I felt no emotional connection.   I was a food dispenser.   I thought Baby could care less where her food was coming from, as long as she was getting fed; I was convinced she didn't know me as Momma. In her eyes was a blank stare. Baby was too young to focus on anything, and I was too lonely to go without eye contact...

You see, I am a woman who relies heavily on what people's eyes tell me.   Excitement, desire, fascination, attentiveness, love, uneasiness, disappointment, contempt—all of these can be found in a person's eyes. If I look carefully enough, clear or red, yellow milkiness, steady or suspicious shiftiness can tell me many things about the depth of one's character.   Love and admiration of a friend.   Purity and honesty of a stranger. Unadulterated joy and confidence in a child. Eyes tell many stories and few lies.

I intentionally surround myself with people with clear, kind eyes. Every now and then there are a few who stand out from the rest—a particular integrity, innocence, and compassion glimmers through, sometimes like a soft caress or maybe a stern grasp. I look at their eyes and they look at mine and we both feel like we could stay there forever. Chaste? Romantic? Maybe neither. Maybe both. Whatever the case, an unmistakable connection is made. But neither of us names it since we are too afraid that in the naming, the connection will fade.

Sometimes I am unable to look into a person's eyes because the death I see is too heavy to hold. I often keep secrets about how miserable I feel when I look at such a person, and make the mistake of holding their agony a second too long. When I see the spoiled pulp of their eyes, I purge myself of their poison and cry a sound that no one should ever hear—a sound akin to a mother wailing over her child's casket. I have convulsed in the midst of tears until everything has been released. I am an impath of some sort. I am sensitive to people's eyes and hence their energy, so I must be careful whose eyes I rest in.

I thought I could find a resting place in Baby's eyes. There was vacancy in those black diamonds and yet no room for me to rest. In all my years of teaching, volunteering at soup kitchens, and counseling at women's shelters, I had the audacity to think I knew what it meant to be selfless. At most, these things made for a good training ground for parenthood. During those two weeks, I learned truly what it meant to be selfless and had a feeling the older she'd become, the more I'd learn. I was feeding her milk from my body without receiving anything in return, not even a loving look—my first lesson in sacrifice. I needed her eyes to feel connected, to prevent myself from feeling isolated. And yet, it was vital that I temporarily set aside this need until she gained focus. My single responsibility was to keep Baby from dying.

There's a fine line between keeping something from dying and keeping something alive. Attitude is the difference. Our perception of the power we possess as women is the difference. Since I had no concrete awareness of how rich and fertile the feminine spirit was, I viewed the milk from the breasts of this first-time Mom as merely a substance—a substance without which an infant would perish.

Not only did my breastmilk keep her from dying, it drew out a golden hue that glowed from her nut brown skin.

This milk kept her alive and healthy, giving her all the nourishment she needed. This miraculous nectar healed the scratches on her face and forced her little baby acne to vanish. It even soothed the sores on my nipples. I kept her alive, and when she finally focused on me for the first time, *she* kept *me* alive. Her stare while nursing or waking from a good nap made me feel like her eyes were all I needed. Baby's black diamonds told me I was complete, enough, and okay.

♪

Baby was almost eight months old, and I was invited to do a presentation on entrainment at New York University. It was my first talk in over a year, and I felt a bit rusty. Nonetheless, I jumped on a plane to New York with a stop in Chicago to deliver one of the most definitive talks of my career.

My breasts were already full by the time I landed in Chicago. I went to the restroom to try out my new breast pump. My original plan was to test it out before the trip, but I was in too much of a hurry. All I could think about was doing whatever necessary to avoid bringing my Medela pump on the trip; I feared airport security would mistake it for a bomb. That thing was too damn expensive for me to risk having it confiscated in the name of homeland security.

Stepping foot in a bathroom stall, I took the thing out and placed it on my left breast. It didn't work. Placed it on the other breast (as if my left breast had malfunctioned). Still didn't work. *I knew I should've brought my good pump!* I muttered to myself, nearly throwing the worthless thing in the toilet. I looked down at my breasts, wondering how much worse the pain would get in two or three hours.

I stood staring in the bathroom mirror. Eyes bloodshot. Breasts engorged. It was 11:00 p.m., and I was in desperate need of sleep and a breast pump. I left the bathroom and walked down the long, wide corridor like Sean Penn approaching his death in *Dead Man Walking.* The milk throbbed within me, creeping across my chest like needles floating in molten lava. The pain transformed into a dull ache that spread throughout my whole body and after awhile I grew numb, still walking, still hoping for some options.

A courtesy desk stood about 20 feet before me, and I heard a host of cherubim and seraphim strumming harps. I prayed like hell that I lived in a world where breast pumps lay somewhere in the dusty recesses of airport storage rooms. I searched the counter for a female face. Someone who would understand. Someone who looked like Mom material. Never mind the man behind the counter, standing there looking happy and helpful; I didn't want to inspire any fantasies of the shape and size of my breasts—neither of which were relevant at the time.

I approached the woman and leaned over the counter and whispered, "You wouldn't by chance have a breast pump would you?"

"No, I'm sorry, we don't," shaking her head with sympathy.

"Nowhere?" I persisted. She continued to shake her head.

I was disappointed. I was hurt. I was hurting. And pissed! Why the hell was I whispering?! And why didn't I feel free enough to speak openly to a man about the presence of a breast pump?! All because I feared being responsible for planting sexual thoughts into his brain?! What kind of twisted world do I live in?!

Peering at the counter, I swear I became Jesus ready to knock that shit over, the same way he flipped over tables in the temple.

This nation, the embodiment of both the puritanical and the hypersexualized, is a place where women's breasts are objects of sexual desire and virtually nothing else. Forget about how breasts provide food for babies and heal the acne and scratches on their little newborn faces. None of this matters to a male-identified world where men and women together obsess over the appearance and exposure of breasts as opposed to the lives they sustain. At what point did women's breasts become so warped, objectified, dissected, and demonized that even mainstream discourse about breastmilk, breastfeeding, and breast pumps became laced with disgust and shame. This shame is so heavy, and it isn't even mine to bear.

Though I teach physics now, I taught history throughout my twenties and challenged students to understand the nature and impact of patriarchy. We engaged in many discussions and debates about the topic. However, it wasn't until my breasts were full in an airport (where there was no trace of a breast pump) that I began to understand how quietly patriarchy operates and yet how deeply it injures the bodies and minds of women and men. In that moment, I wondered how many other women in that airport were engorged and in pain just like me.

I started again toward my gate. The faces of passers-by were a blur as I daydreamt about a room filled with breast pumps where a Mother could walk up to one of ten stalls and pump her excess milk. Each stall would have a Medela dual breast pump and a dispenser for disposable breastshields and tubing.   Now, it would be ideal if this was free, but I pictured putting a quarter or fifty cents into the pump and getting about five minutes worth of pumping—something comparable to filling up your tires at a gas station or vacuuming your car at a carwash. This milk would be bottled, screened, and then delivered to cities throughout the world where infants were starving for breastmilk.   It would be very easy. So, why don't these exist? Donor milk banks already exist.   How difficult would it be to create a partnership between airports and donor milk banks around the world to ensure that pumped milk from airports would be distributed to caregivers of infants that the banks have established contact with. We have safe surrenders for mothers who want to drop off their unwanted children within the first three days of life. Why not have one more means by which these infants can have access to milk?   Why don't we see billboards for breastmilk pumping rooms? Or ads in magazines—and not just in magazines strictly focused on parenthood. Have them in Newsweek, The Oprah Magazine, Vibe, GQ, Glamour, and Wired. Now that we have more commercials that come on before our favorite YouTube videos and shows on Hulu, picture commercials for a breastmilk pumping room. Let's call the room, "The Breastmilk Express." The name is shameless, explicit, and fun. No need for sterile euphemisms like "Women's Rest Area." No!

But what if, by chance "The Breastmilk Express" creates too much of a rift in the mainstream psyche; we could simply call it, "Expressions for Mothers"—soft and classy, with a bit of a shopping mall feel. Whatever the case, the name should communicate the room's purpose. I had it all figured out and prayed that "The Breastmilk Express" or "Expressions for Mothers" would somehow miraculously appear next to the Interfaith chapel I was sitting in. It never did.

I remained in pain until I arrived at my hotel room. I got out of the cab and stood, looking up at the Millenium Broadway Hotel. Tall and stately. Glossy. Black. I stood in front of its beige entrance, smiling at its torch-like lamps, enamored with the building's beauty. As I stepped through the automatic doors, for a split second, I forgot about the pain I was in. I checked in and then immediately ran up to my room, thinking about how soothing a warm bath would feel.

It was 2:45 a.m., and I sat in the warm tub in disbelief. Gently massaging my breasts, I saw swirls of breastmilk disappear into the depth of the bathwater. I kept massaging and squeezing. And more breastmilk came out. Relief. I didn't think relief would be possible during this trip. I sat in awe of what my female body could do, very much in the same way I was fascinated with how a woman's body transforms during pregnancy. I learned from my body that night. I discovered that I could express milk by hand. And for the next two days, I expressed my milk once every two hours.

و

Yawning in the back of Schwartz Hall, I waited for Dr. Foyle Mallard to finish up his presentation on entrainment. Mallard was just as insufferable as everyone said he was. Yet in this world of academia, any contempt academics have for each other is silenced if the professor can fool you into believing in his brilliance. And that was good ol' Mallard.

This man's voice—intellectual assault. His presence—a slow kind of calculated homicide. Torture is listening to a professor talk about your favorite subject as if he was delivering a eulogy. It was difficult to tell if his talk served as a good sedative to take my mind off the pain or if his arrogance just gave me something more painful to focus on.

His talk was my cue to run to the restroom while I could. My presentation was in 20 minutes.

In the bathroom. Again. Expressing my own breastmilk was the most excruciating self-inflicted act I had ever performed. Doing it over a toilet seemed tragic. I was closed off from the world in the cold metal privacy of a bathroom stall where piss and feces were swallowed up by some white contraption planted in the floor. There I was, squeezing Baby's food into the same contraption—because I had no choice. My human dignity lay trapped somewhere between my heart and the door of that stall, wondering if anyone could bear witness to the glory of my womanhood now.

I returned to my seat, somewhat relieved, but a bit sore. Within minutes, I hear, "Thank you, Dr. Foyle Mallard for that enlightening exploration of the relationship between entrainment and full coherence. Our next speaker is Dr. Gold Taraji, professor of quantum physics at the University of Illinois at Urbana-Champaign, delivering a presentation entitled, "Entrainment—The Key to Mending Hearts."

I stood up: bright smile, chest out, breasts empty. Relaxed and excited all at once. Light applause filled the room, and I stepped forward and began my presentation. The words flowed out like syrup, but the audience seemed closed and stoic. I scanned the room and found a few friendly faces. At academic conferences, smiling faces in an audience are those parents sitting in the stands, cheering on their child at a soccer game. I live for those faces because they've always carried me during my talks. Luckily, those kind faces were there as I continued.

"Let's consider two things: resonant frequency and entrainment. McTaggart, in *The Intention Experiment*, describes resonant frequency as the preferential frequencies at which any vibrating thing finds vibrating easiest. And most of us are familiar with entrainment being the phenomenon of two oscillating bodies falling into sync. Huygens coined this concept in 1665 when he took two pendulums, each swinging at different rates, placed them close to each other and discovered that over time, they began to swing at the same rate. This is entrainment. What if we applied this to humans? Each human being has her/his own vibration that s/he is most comfortable vibrating at. If we bring two people together, entrainment can also happen. The research of Grinberg-Zylberbaum and Ramos offers compelling evidence of this. They found that the person with the most cohesive or most ordered quantum wave patterns had a tendency to influence the wave patterns of the other person. If you are more 'ordered' you can set the rhythm for the other person. You can change someone else's vibration. So imagine if you invest your energy in being generous, loving and honest. Your very presence can create change in another person on a subatomic level, causing them to do the same! If you are strong enough and consistent enough, people almost can't help but be captivated and influenced by your glow! So the question becomes, how do we become more 'ordered'?"

People were turning around, leaning toward each other, whispering. Some leaned forward. Others straightened up in their seats. I paused for a moment until everything settled down. The audience was mine. Their eyes told me they were right there with me. My spirit rose as I saw more smiles and felt the new energy in the room. I wanted to revel in the excitement of the moment, but little did they know that my breasts were filling up by the minute, so we needed to move things along. Using my Iphone, I switched slides...

_9_

The cab driver waved to me as I thanked him for the conversation. I dragged my luggage into the airport and checked in. I couldn't wait to get home. I was worried that Baby was close to running out of the breastmilk I pumped for her. I missed Baby and the pain in my breasts was a physical reminder. I missed Sterling. My love. He sounded so worried on the phone, but he still reassured me that everything would be alright.

I had dinner at a fast food Chinese restaurant: some sweet and sour chicken, fried rice and chow mein—what I normally eat when I have Chinese food. I figured if I ate before the flight, I wouldn't starve on the plane. But after inhaling the food in fear that I'd miss my flight, I found myself sitting on the plane, feeling my stomach rumble. Then, a fever. Food poisoning. Shit! Can anything else happen?

Our plane was late getting into Chicago. I rushed to the gate for my connecting flight to Champaign, thinking the pilot might wait. No such luck. The plane left. The next flight for Champaign: 6:30 a.m. the following morning. The airport and every single one of its restrooms became my home that night.

In the baggage claim area, I spread myself across a couple of chairs (with arm rests), hoping to get a little sleep as I kept one eye open and held a pen in my fist just in case someone tried something funny. I found creative ways of making sure no one would steal my belongings, using my backpack as both pillow and leg rest.

Yeah, sleep was tricky that night. When fluorescent lights are shining in your eyes, your breasts are engorged, and food poisoning calls you to the restroom every 15 minutes, the most one could do is sit still and let your dreams take you elsewhere. All I could think about was being with my family in a warm bed and drinking my favorite watermelon drink from this snack shop near 99 Ranch.

When this dream was interrupted by the discomfort of the chairs and the frequent trips to the bathroom to express milk, answer nature's call, or do both, I drug myself from my makeshift bed to go take care of business.

I Ate My Placenta

first two weeks after Baby's birth

felt lifeless

disconnected

afraid

peeled off the membrane of my placenta

boiled it in ginger and onions

diced it

put it in some lasagna

pasta sauce
lasagna noodle
pasta sauce
ricotta cheese
diced placenta
lasagna noodle
sauce
ricotta
placenta
noodle
sauce
shredded cheese

and bake

first couple bites

what did it taste like?

not sure

i held my breath

few more bites

took a breath

what did it taste like?

regular lasagna with meat

meat: the texture of liver and gizzard combined

six days later

oxytocin levels up

feeling alive again

unafraid

One Child, One Punch Later
A Journal Entry

> I don't know who you are. I don't know what you
> want. If you are looking for ransom, I can tell you
> I don't have money. But what I do have are a very
> particular set of skills; skills I have acquired over a
> very long career. Skills that make me a nightmare
> for people like you. If you let my daughter go
> now, that'll be the end of it. I will not look for
> you, I will not pursue you. But if you don't, I will
> look for you, I will find you, and I will kill you.[2]

Liam Neeson is hard, I thought as I watched *Taken*. He played Bryan in that movie and his words were as calm as they were threatening. For the first time, I was confronted with the possibility of my 16-month-old daughter being in danger. I realized that if anyone tried to physically harm her, I couldn't defend her, protect her, rescue her.

That month, I decided to take up Muay Thai—a martial art referred to as the Science of Eight Limbs.

❧

I walked into a Muay Thai gym in Oakland for the first time and was slightly nervous. Everyone looked so tough. Kicking heavy bags. Sparring in the ring. Jumping rope. Shadowboxing. This environment was totally foreign to me.

---

[2] *Taken*, directed by Pierre Morel (2008; Los Angeles, CA: 20th Century Fox Film Corporation, 2009), DVD.

And when I'm in a foreign environment, I shut up, pay attention and follow instructions. Much of what I was exposed to during the traditional class reminded me of running track and playing in the marching band in high school. Luckily, I could draw from the discipline I learned back then to remain focused and unflappable in the face of stern instructions. When the awkward feeling became too much, I invoked these lessons learned from track and band. The fact that I was in a gym where Biggie, Tribe, and Pharcyde were playing in the background also calmed me down. Maybe this place wasn't so foreign after all.

All the hang-ups I had reconciling physical violence with prayer, childrearing, and peace came to a crossroads in that space. At this gym, I noticed the instructors and the students in the traditional class had already come to terms with these things. They brought their children to watch, train, and tumble. Cheetah, the owner at the time, always welcomed me by name and showed an interest in me as an individual. He reminded me that Muay Thai was a fighting art *and* a lifestyle. I remember in theology school, my professors would call this ability to give attention to everyone you come in contact with, "Being pastoral."

Alex was my first teacher. He was encouraging and gave me the space to make mistakes. Alex never intervened too soon to correct every single missed form, but he did intervene soon enough so mistakes wouldn't become permanent.

Linda was another instructor at the gym. Though I didn't have much experience training with her, I had the impression that she was well-respected for being a no-bullshit-type of teacher. She seemed like a serious hard-ass and to be honest, she kinda scared me. She had no interest in complaints. Determination won her respect (as with all the instructors). And what I loved the most was that Linda was deeply affectionate with the kids who regularly came to the gym.

Ra gave regular spiels about it being National Hygiene Month—every month. They'd begin a little something like this: "Before you come to the gym, you need to bathe and use deodorant!" And to the men in the room, he'd remind them, "Put the toilet seat down!"

When Ra would say things like, "In the ring you do it this way, but in the streets you do it like this," or "I don't know what you really call this drill, but in the penitentiary they call it *la maquina,*" I thought, *Damn, who am I talkin' to right now?* But truly, these things were good for me to hear, even though they were a bit jarring for someone who'd never been in a fight before.

Ra had a talent for weaving profound lessons into every class. I remember one had to do with upper cuts: "It's not always about power; sometimes it's about economy of motion and being able to reach your target using the shortest distance." I can't tell you how many times I've applied this to my personal and professional life.

As I continued training with Ra, I eventually learned that in addition to being a Muay Thai fighter and instructor, he was a former fourth grade teacher, is a historian and sociologist by nature, and owns a daycare.

These instructors give people the skills, the tools to defeat the fear within. With each punch and kick, they have empowered their students. Like most good teachers, they don't take credit for the empowerment their students feel.

Muay Thai has changed the way I walk in the world. It has improved my reflexes. It has slowly given me alternatives. In a confrontation, I don't have to be silent or polite. I don't have to run. I have another option: I can stay and fight.

But first, I need to practice...practice enough so that every push kick-jab-cross, every roundhouse-jab-cross-upper cut will be locked into my body. Automatic. Muscle memory formed.

❧

Muay Thai has kept me honest. During my first month of training, I was practicing a jab-cross-1-2-1-2 combination with either an instructor or one of the advanced students...I can't remember. Even when I had a clear shot for his head, I chose to hit his gloves instead. He said, "Why you keep hittin' my glove? Why you keep hittin' my glove?"

I said, "I don't know. I don't know." So finally when he gave me an open shot for his head, I hit him.

"Oh, my God, I'm so sorry!"

"That's good. That's good!" he said.

My heart immediately filled up, and I felt it in my throat. Tears fell from the corners of my eyes. I played it off like it was sweat, "Ah, I got sweat in my eyes, hold on a second. Okay, okay, I'm ready. I'm ready." But I knew I'd have to think about this. Why did I cry after hitting someone?

I realized that I'd never intentionally hurt anyone before (except for in the 8th grade when I put a boy in a headlock for about 30 minutes because he kept messin' with my hair). Okay, so throughout most of my life, I'd never deliberately hit, kicked, shot, or stabbed anyone. I've also tried not to use my words like daggers or ammunition. I had always been so careful, perhaps too careful...that even when speaking my truth, I'd try my best to spare a person's feelings in the process.

I had never inflicted violence in any form: physical or verbal...and now I find myself in the ring, training to accurately strike my target, fast and hard—a task so counter to my natural inclination. No wonder. No wonder I started to cry. I guess this means I need to go back into the ring on Monday...to learn how to be, as Bryan said, a "nightmare" for anyone who thinks about harming my daughter.

Meeting the Sky
(From Jumper to Jumper)

Peel away the wind
Push it behind.
Blurred sceneries punctuated by nondescript faces
     I see
          stop
             and watch.
Palms open
     Quads rippling, dripping sweat
Blood pulsing
     This is my day.

My muscles hold the memory of yesterday, but
The rush stifles remnants of shin splints and sore muscles.

Press on.
     This is my day.
Left foot plants,
     Springs below
          Recoil and release
             And I see only baby blue and wisps
of white
             As my chest is strung up by harp
strings
                Telling me to come
closer

My soul connects with the Sky,

I fly
Absent of thought
My body knows the rest
Mechanics become automatic
Legs bicycle beneath
Arms circle 'round for trees
No longer beyond reach.
I swing from branches to know the Sky
just a little bit longer
And ride the spring breeze
like rip curls.
The Pit can wait.

Adrenalin pulls me until I can go no higher.
I hover still for a split second
To visit Sister Dragonfly and Lady Hummingbird
And play in this invisible cradle—
my home before birth.

But my second home calls out to me
And I fall slowly
Eyes closed
I know
There beneath
The Pit waits for me.
Dark brown, soft Earth
Cool, anxious

And I land.
My feet disappear

          Spikes enveloped by sand so quick
My land cushioned
          Grains splash from the Pit

I step out. Silent.
No words for what I saw, what I felt.

I can only let the measurement
          Tell you
I met the Sky.

Inspired by the Salesian High School Long and Triple Jumpers
Spring 2004

Blood Orange Drops

Blood orange drops in the corners of your mouth and I
wonder if that's juice.
Or is it the blood of your ancestors pimped out for personal
politics.

You leech, you parasite!
And you wonder why people spit in your face.
You can't claim pride without visiting us, without listening to
us.
You can't claim support without sacrifice.

You dare flaunt your degrees as if they matter to us.
Your diplomas, resume, books
Are worth nothing here.
Our lives are not your credentials.
How dare you use our names in vain!

Slither a little closer,
Let me tell you a secret...
Don't forget in the end you answer to us.
You have no idea how powerful we are, do you?

Don't ever speak my name before you wipe my gravestone
and bring me stargazers,
Hipon at kamatis,
Avocadoes with ice and condensed milk
Dugo dugo and one coconut shell filled with *tuba*,
Light a candle and pray the novena each year I die and die

again.

Don't speak my name and then tip past our graves, our trees, our anthills without saying, "*Tabi tabi, po.*"

Because make no mistake,
Give me ungrateful guests, and I'll make 'em grateful.

Let this be your warning.

But for now:
May the Holy Spirit keep you
Hold you in her arms
So all you know is love
And all you share is love
May these words be sealed with your tears and mine.
Your blood and mine.

Ashe.

Hell's Body

I wonder who he was...what he was like. I mean, I'd heard of him, but this was the first time I'd actually seen him. He looked like a fairly young man. Too young and handsome to think he was ill. Though the weight of gravity pulled on his every limb, making even his cheeks fall limp, his body still seemed tense as if he changed his mind at the last minute or as if the pain he sought to escape had followed him into the afterlife. The air had a foul stench not caused by his body. It smelled like despair—a despair telling the story of a man misunderstood. A man who didn't understand himself. An infant soul trapped in a man's body, reluctantly accepting adult responsibilities. The story of a man whose eloquence convinced everyone he was courageous, when in truth, he possessed a trembling spirit that caused him to fear the dangerous, avoid eye contact with the pure. It wasn't violence he feared, or people with questionable character. He feared what I call truth tellers, what he called liars.

The stench tells me he was a childhood loner who took twisted pleasure in being a dick. Battered, mad dog. An only child who stayed occupied by crouching over puddles, drowning fire ants, watching them frantically flounder, only to be their savior, reaching out a stick that they quickly grabbed onto. For a brief moment, he was proud of himself. But this satisfaction quickly turned into rage when he realized the ants did not know they owed their lives to him. So he crushed them. Still dissatisfied.

He believed this world wasn't ready for him and that maybe it would be ready later. He never stopped to think that maybe he had much to learn from the world and his enemies. He believed he was harmless and selfless. At the same time, he hated himself and hated all who reminded him of his flaw—his inability to tell the truth.

His friends, lovers, enemies should have seen it coming. Toward the end, he couldn't contain the evil that corroded his spirit. He lashed out at everything and everyone, especially me. I was the woman he secretly admired and publicly despised. Judging from his book reviews and comments on different blogs, he couldn't stand my work or me. I disgusted him. In his mind, I exposed what he tried so hard to hide. And this was enough to cause him to end his torment permanently.

The air told me many things. The air helped me make sense of the hearsay. Though I have done this work for many years, this was the first time I felt the depth of the person's despair and yet felt no pity.

Spirit

When I'm around her, I feel like my energy is being scrambled. Ordinarily, I'm a pretty clear thinker…fairly articulate. However, when she's near me, I can't think straight. I feel unintelligent and unprepared. I know I'm not stupid. So why do I sound so stupid? And only around her! It's not like she's overtly domineering or exceedingly charismatic…not all that sexy or confident either—qualities that usually make me slightly self-conscious and cause me to fumble a bit.

I know she's always in a hurry. She can't sit still…always doing something with her hands or tapping her feet. She sounds agitated all the time. Everything she says and does complicates situations more than necessary. Seems like there's some undercurrent of condescension in her tone, too. This woman: she hides well. Yeah, she's good at hiding. Multiple disguises this woman has; I suspect she's lived in fear most of her life.

It wasn't until I took a job somewhere else—a place where I was surrounded by healthier people—that it occurred to me: this woman had very strong disruptive, unsettling energy that created some static in my thought process. It deeply affected my ability to communicate and interact with others in a way that reflected my most authentic self.

I offered to cleanse some classrooms today. For the most part it was meditative and centering, but after an hour, I regretted it. I was tired, anxious, and hungry. I cursed God for the very size of these rooms. I was just about to call it a day and do the rest tomorrow when at the last minute I decided to do one more.

I walked into a fairly plain, nondescript classroom. It didn't really appear aesthetically pleasing. Desks were in standard block formation. Nothing on the walls besides dry erase boards. No plants around. No indoor fountains or things like that. No windows.

But something strange happened. Within seconds of walking in, I calmed down. I wanted to lie down right in the middle of the floor and just stay. I proceeded to cleanse the space and thanked God for allowing me to feel such a beautiful energy.

A few days later, I learned that the two professors who teach in that room are incredibly patient and approachable. Both are friendly and gentle in their own way. They have a calming influence that allows them to draw out the best work from their students. I didn't know that such people could leave behind their essence in a room. Hmm. So…goodness is strong.

They Speak

Momma calls me and says nothing.
I say, "Hello."
She only cries with a deep agony
I hadn't heard in years.
I just listen.

The next day, the Twin Towers fall.

Our house is on fire and Daddy stands knee-deep in water,
holding a bucket.
Daddy takes bucket after bucket of water to put out the fire,
but the water is not enough.
The water keeps coming
And yet the fire burns.

The next day, the tsunami hit.

If Momma really called and Daddy really tried
putting out that fire
These would be ordinary stories.

> But when I woke up, I remembered
> Momma and Daddy had been dead for years.

That morning, I stopped wondering if spirits mourn when
thousands of people leave this world to join theirs.

> I stopped wondering if spirits speak to those they love
> as long as we want to listen.

But then I wonder why my parents didn't warn me before
Katrina and Rita came over.

No phone call, no flooded, burning house.

Did Momma run out of tears?

Was Daddy's house so flooded
there was no room for more water?

Or were these hurricanes, these floods, this deliberate neglect,
all so bad that even spirits were at a loss of what to say.

All of this
So unbelievable
Their rage and sorrow tied themselves into some thick
knot, waiting to be unraveled by time, to make
themselves comprehensible to the human spirit.

I don't know.
But I will sit and wait until they speak.
Knowing that next time I won't be the only one to hear them.

Midnight Peaches, Two O'Clock Patience

Midnight peaches, in a fog of sleep
Two o'clock patience.
That's all she needed.

"Apple Jacks in milk with a spoon in a bowl," she says.
"Milk in a cup with the top," she says.

And two hours later,
Four hours later,
She falls asleep, watching Scooby Doo.
Wakes up, fighting kids with Spiderman webs.

But with a cup of peaches, she falls asleep right away.

I thought I was patient before having a child.
But I'm not.
Baby teaches me:
"Midnight peaches, two o'clock patience.
That's all I need Mommy."

Eat With Your Hands

Food tastes better with your hands.

Taste isn't just in the mouth. Taste is in the body.
Taste is an experience, a memory of home and comfort.
It's family. It's familiar. It's culture.

As I sit at the table,
       one foot resting on a chair,
               legs spread,
                    hunched over a
                bowl of steamed rice and
                ham,
I eat with my hands.

Eating with my hands is how I stay connected to Momma.

I learned to eat with my hands by watching her.
Momma's hand was graceful in the plate,
            making a quick "S," squeezing rice and
            mackerel between her fingers.

I could never do it quite right.
Food fell all over my hands and down to my elbows.

Eating with your hands requires practice.
The same practice it takes to use a spoon.

And with practice

And later watching

       Tita squeezing rice and *bagoong* together and

Tito squeezing rice and chicken together,
one foot on the chair.

I eat now

I eat now with my hands

And I'm good.

Ham and rice

Hot dogs and rice

Eggs and rice

Spaghetti and rice

I eat it all with my hands

And I remember

I come from a long line of Filipinos
Filipinos who never thought themselves savage for
Eating with their hands.

I look across the table
Baby eats rice and ham with her hands,
Looking at me with happy eyes
And I am proud.

When her bowl is empty
She asks for more
I squeeze rice and ham together

And put it in her mouth
She opens wide like a baby bird
My heart beats fast
My Love
My Baby
My Sunshine

She relies on my hands.
Her generation gets fed
By our hands.

Let us not forget.

Feeding the Dead, the Young, & the Unborn
A Reflection on Ethnic Studies

Twenty-three years ago in a nursing home in Lancaster, CA, I looked across a dining room table and saw my father trying to feed himself. He placed phantom spoonfuls of mashed potatoes and peas in his mouth. His hands weren't steady enough to scoop up the food, and all that landed in his mouth was the idea of dinner. I gently took the spoon, scooped up some mashed potatoes and peas and fed my father for the first time. I was 15 years old then, and the decision to feed him came quite naturally since this was the same man who fed me when I was a child.

This wasn't the last time I fed my father. I fed him many times before he died, and many times after he died.

Each time I learned something new about his/my/our ancestors—our African and African American history, I was fed. And each time I passed on this knowledge, I was feeding him. The stories he told, the words he used gained new meaning with every moment I learned about the cultural context that shaped my father's experience. No longer were his words the incoherent ramblings of an old man; they became cultural artifacts situated in a specific time and place in history.

For example, when someone said something surprising, Daddy would say, "Now das' a whoopin' boy right there!"—

the "whoopin' boy" being a duppy or a spirit lying deep within the roots of cotton trees.[3]

Daddy's memories of hopping freight trains from Shreveport, Louisiana to Texas, and then from Texas to California was one story among millions—a story finding its place in the Great Migration when six million African-Americans between 1915 and 1970 left the oppression of the South for other parts of the United States.[4]

I am fortunate enough to find myself teaching an Africana Studies course where I can share these stories and more. Whether I learn or teach Africana Studies, I am feeding my father the way I fed him in the nursing home.

I am pouring libation—a ritual practiced throughout the continent of Africa, involving the pouring of water, wine, beer, or milk into the Earth to remember and remain in communion with the deceased.[5] It is a way to honor and remain connected to the dead.

To not remember the deceased through libation or the laying out of food is to condemn them to a state of non-existence

---

[3] Rebecca Tortello, "The Fall of a Gentle Giant—The Collapse of Tom Cringle's Cotton Tree," *Jamaica Gleaner,* February 25, 2002, accessed October 15, 2004, http://www.jamaica-gleaner.com/pages/history/story0020.html.
[4] Isabel Wilkerson, *The Warmth of Other Sons: The Epic Story of America's Great Migration* (New York: Random House, 2010), 9.
[5] John S. Mbeti, *African Religions and Philosophy* (London: Heinemann Educational Books, 1988), 26.

which is believed to be the worst possible punishment for anyone…including the dead.[6]

Through Africana Studies, through all Ethnic Studies courses, we are remembering the ancestors and remaining in communion with them. It is our libation. And through libation we feed and sustain the ancestors so they can remain strong enough to feed us with their guidance.[7] So when we feed them, they feed us.

Through the wisdom we gain, our intellects and spirits are being fed—the ancestors feed us with the wisdom they have left behind. And then we give thanks by pouring more water into the Earth. And so the cycle continues…as long as there is no interference.[8]

☙

As a professor of Ethnic Studies, I have witnessed the empowering impact of Ethnic Studies on students of color and white students alike.

Such courses create greater understanding of the multidimensional experiences of marginalized ethnic groups in

---

[6] Ibid., 27.

[7] Wade Nobles, personal communication with author, San Francisco State University, February 2005.

[8] This piece is a selection adapted from my presentation entitled, "Africana Studies as Libation" which was delivered at Napa Valley College on December 1, 2011. This talk was part of the "Emerging Voices in Academia" Speaker Series sponsored by the Associated Students of Napa Valley College.

the United States and help promote and improve intercultural communication and relationships, benefitting all students.

By learning about Ethnic Studies, we are engaging in a liberatory practice that frees us from cultural amnesia and allows us to live out our fullest potential.

Ethnic Studies defies the systematic erasure of Latina(o)s, African-Americans, Native-Americans, Asian Pacific Islander-Americans, and Arab-Americans—people who lived yesterday, people who live today, and people who **will live** tomorrow.

In the process of engaging in this liberatory act, when students of color learn about the history that was kept from them, they become connected to their ancestors and free to recognize them as active, creative, inventive, and resilient agents in the shaping of history, as well as in the shaping of the present and the future.

This discipline situates people of color in history so we are not rendered invisible, destitute, pathological, primitive, or starving and instead are recognized for our hand in shaping the United States—attention given to our heroes, scholars, warriors, healers, and inventors.

It gives meaning to our own lives and the lives of those we love.

One of the things I've noticed when students learn about their ethnic heritage and the legacy of excellence amongst their ancestors is that they become motivated to excel in subjects like math, science, english, and history. There is a link between the existence of Ethnic Studies and courses that have been characterized as "core courses." Truly neither can survive without the other.

It has a tremendous influence on students' ability to envision themselves graduating from high school and college, pursuing the profession of their dreams, impacting the world, and transforming lives.

In addition to this, as they find their anchor, they become inspired to learn about other ethnicities…and so the interethnic, intercultural, interracial bonds get stronger and stronger.

For all people, Ethnic Studies is a reminder that our stories are central to the fabric of the United States…not a threat to national security or a threat to integration. Nor is it something cute and sexy but unnecessary. Ethnic Studies is and will continue to be essential.

To our sisters and brothers in the Tuscon Unified School District, as you face HB 2281, banning public schools in Arizona from teaching Ethnic Studies, please know you have family right here in the Napa Valley who stand in solidarity with you, right along with all teachers and students of Ethnic

Studies across the nation, serving to create a shift in consciousness to bring about greater human connection.[9]

---

[9] This piece is an adaptation of an introductory speech delivered on May 3, 2012 at the Napa Valley College screening of *Precious Knowledge*—an event hosted and organized by the Napa Valley Ethnic Studies Advocates.

Locks

In my twenties, I used to lean over the side of the bathtub, putting relaxer in my hair, straightening out the new growth every two to three weeks. The instructions said to wait 20-25 minutes before rinsing it out. I didn't bother following the instructions. Instead, I waited 35 minutes until I felt my scalp burn, until I felt the perfect pain. When I couldn't stand it any longer, I washed the relaxer out. I wanted to make sure it turned out just right: straight enough so you couldn't see the naps, but wavy enough so you could still tell I was Black.

I relaxed my hair for the last time in my early thirties. Something was different that final time leaning over the tub. Usually when I poured the neutralizer over my scalp and shampooed my hair, my scalp would stop hurting—an indication that the relaxer was fully washed out. This time my scalp continued to sting and burn. Sitting there on the bathroom floor, I began to question why I put myself through so much pain to keep Africa from shining through. I began reflecting upon larger questions about complicity—how I participate in keeping systems of hatred in place—how I reinforce notions of inferiority, pathology, and deficiency about all of us of African descent.

What kind of silent contempt did I harbor against myself and the hair I was born with—the hair of my father, my aunties and uncles, my grandparents, and all the great-grandparents and great-great-grandparents that I had never met but had known me long before I was born. I see them praying that I would never know the prisons that kept them from living and blossoming, the prisons that were so afraid of their strength, intellect, and spirit that they were kept contained, isolated, mentally and physically shackled, their gifts hidden from themselves and from the world.

And these prisons,

these prisons,

they haven't disappeared.

◊

June 2005, I decided to lock my hair and go Natural.

I wanted my scalp to heal from 18 years of chemicals,
conformity,
and self-hatred.

I hoped to embrace these locks as a
spiritual lifeline to my ancestors.

I wanted to *be* Natural
and by returning to the Natural and the
Unforced, I hoped to
deepen my connection to
my Source, my Creator.

I started with a little over an inch of new growth. That modest, untainted sprig of hair was twisted and twisted with shea butter everyday. And for the first time, I learned from my hair and heard something that it was trying to tell me for over two decades: *I am multiple textures.* Mostly coarse, but soft and fine near my forehead, around my ears, and near the nape of my neck; it was softest at my crown. I never knew this about my own hair until I stopped putting chemicals in it. Originally, I was told to expect my hair to lock in about six months, but since my hair was so soft and fine in certain areas, it took about a year and a half to lock completely.

Unfortunately, the man who twisted my hair, James, didn't understand that his own people could have different textures throughout their hair, especially those of us who were multiracial. He also didn't understand how important moisturizer was for my scalp. Even though he advised me to wash my hair once a month to allow the locks to stay in, I still washed my hair once a week because the itching was unbearable; even washing it once a week was torture since I was accustomed to washing it far more frequently. As time went on, I discovered the main reason why my scalp became itchy so quickly was because 18-years-worth of chemicals had damaged my scalp, making it incredibly dry. Throughout this time, I never moisturized my scalp. Essentially, I was undergoing a detoxification process and had to nurture my hair and scalp with plenty of moisturizing nutrients so my scalp and hair could become healthy again. With each visit, James noticed I washed my hair which caused many of the twists to wash out.

"Are you afraid to lock your hair? Because if you're afraid you can just tell me. I just need to know. If it's fear that's keepin' you from leaving these locks in…"

"No. I'm not afraid! I want locks. That's why I keep coming back!"

What the hell? He wouldn't let it go. He continued to ask and ask, and I was pissed! Sitting there in the chair, tears welled up in my eyes as he blamed me for some subconscious fear I did not possess. That was the last time I saw James.

The following month I found a shop in Richmond and met Charlene. She had years of experience locking hair and working with people who had multi-textured hair. She explained to me that this was common amongst many of her clients who were mixed. For this reason, she wasn't surprised that it took awhile for my hair to lock; nonetheless, she assured me that it would. I just had to continue twisting it and trying my best to wash it maybe every two to three weeks to give the hair a chance to lock.

◊

It wasn't until I began locking my hair that I realized what Black hair could do. How fascinating that all of us of African descent possess hair capable of locking without the help of chemicals. Never did I think that twisting my hair long enough with shea butter would cause it to remain twisted—the individual strands of hair tangling to create one strong shaft. For most of my life, I couldn't stand the slightest tangle or out-of-place hair that wasn't "tamed" by pomada, mousse, or hair spray. I desperately longed for straight, flowing hair and hated how stiff and coarse my hair was. For over 25 years of my life, coarse hair and tangles were not only undesirable, but disgusting.

Having locks dramatically transformed my self-loathing into self-respect. Consequently, a greater love for my fellow sisters and brothers of African descent was created within me. I no longer detested my hair—our hair. Instead, I realized how versatile Black hair truly was.

Such self-loathing runs far deeper than the sweeping, superficial generalizations made about our "human" inability to be happy with what we're born with. We hear this revealed by dismissive rhetoric like, "No one's ever satisfied with what they have. Black people want straight hair. White people want curly hair. Black people want to be lighter and White people want a tan. The grass is always greener, right?" Wrong! There are systems in place that communicate to the world that long, straight, flowing hair that blows in the wind is the standard against which all other hair types ought to be measured and evaluated. Though it may be true that those with straight and/or limp hair receive the message that having more body or wave to one's hair is more desirable, one must take a close look at how prevalent such messages are in comparison to the implicit and explicit messages (from within and outside our race) that bombard Black women and girls, telling us that straight hair is not only preferable and normative, but anything other than straight is deviant, dirty, messy, and akin to pubic hair. These judgments don't stop at your physical appearance, but they also imply that your inner way of being is just as dirty and deviant. Secondly, there is a big difference between telling women that hair with more body and wave is beautiful and telling women that coarse, kinky, or nappy hair is beautiful. Ads, for example, that implicitly or explicitly promote hair with more body and wave (or maybe even ringlets, too) communicate the message that it's okay to have some waves, but if its too curly and too frizzy, at the same time, you are on the brink of creeping into ugly territory! Such messages are communicated through casual conversation, jokes, silent stares of contempt, magazines, music videos, television, Korean-owned and Black-owned hair supply stores, billboards, cinema, dolls, greeting cards, the Internet, and much more. Never had I researched how to straighten and damage my hair through the use of a chemical relaxer, hairdryer, hot comb, or curling iron. Nonetheless, this came quite naturally to me considering what was readily available; I was provided with plenty of assistance. Over the years, however, becoming aware of how I internalized these destructive external messages put me in a better position to actively choose to reject such messages and begin to understand my hair.

How strange it is to realize that in my thirties I must
***learn* from books**
how to take care of my natural hair.

To learn how to grow long, healthy locks, I first sought the guidance offered in Lonnice Bonner's *Nice Dreads*. Bonner's text was instrumental in teaching me how to care for my locks. I encourage others to do their own research, using suggestions from a variety of texts that work best for your own hair care needs. Indeed, I have benefitted (and continue to benefit) from the comprehensive recommendations Bonner gives in her book.   Experience has also taught me additional ways of taking care of my locks that I would like to share with you.

1. I wash my hair with Dr. Bronner's liquid soap, adding a couple drops of tea tree oil. [10]   In terms of frequency, Bonner recommends washing your locks every five to ten days.[11] This combination cleans all products, dirt and oil from my hair and scalp.[12] I wash it at least twice, scratching away all dirt and dandruff.   Following each wash, I rinse my hair, gently squeezing the water from my locks.

2. Use a black or dark brown towel to dry your hair to avoid the white lint left behind by light-colored towels. Squeeze excess water from your hair.

3. Use pure avocado oil, rich in vitamin E, to condition your hair and scalp.[13] Mix a cup of avocado oil with about five drops of your favorite essential oil. Heat

---

[10] I add the drops of tea tree oil to the liquid soap during every other wash.

[11] Lonnice Bonner, *Nice Dreads: Hair Care Basics and Inspiration for Colored Girls Who've Considered Locking Their Hair* (New York, Three Rivers Press, 2005), 53.

[12] Ibid., 52-85.

[13] Alex Malinsky, "Avocado Oil Circulates with a Healthy Crowd," *Natural News,* last modified March 23, 2011, http://www.naturalnews.com/031801_avocado_oil_healthy_fats.html.

for about 45 seconds. Pour into an applicator bottle. Apply the mixture to your scalp and hair. Massage it in gently, but thoroughly. Applying avocado oil to your hair and scalp daily can keep both moisturized.

4. Wrap your hair in aluminum foil. Make sure your scalp is fully covered and that the foil is tight around your head. Use a plastic grocery bag for a cap, tying the handles tightly at the nape your neck. The heat of your scalp will condition your hair. Leave on for 40 minutes to an hour. Sure, you might look like you're waiting to be abducted by aliens, but who cares. More than likely you'll be doing this at home—a place where hopefully you feel the least self-conscious about your appearance.

5. Remove the bag and foil. Squeeze out excess oil with a dark towel. Twist each lock with melted unrefined shea butter (adding preferred essential oil) and secure each lock with a metal clip. Wrap hair in a black satin or silk scarf and set overnight. An alternative to this is sitting under a dryer for about one hour, and then removing the clips.

6. Decorate your hair by sewing in cowry shells and beads. Enjoy your locks. Watch them shine in the sun. Style your locks in ways that fit your personality. Let your locks be a vibrant reflection of the beautiful things taking place within your soul.

7. Be firm and set boundaries preventing random people from touching your hair. Remember that your locks are your glory. Your hair can be admired, but you are not a lab specimen, pet, or a strange foreign object. Know that people who touch your hair without your permission are assuming familiarity. Sometimes this is also an expression of a person's wonder and fascination. Whatever the case, when a stranger assumes that touching your hair (or any other part of your body) does not require your consent, this is a violation. This is one manifestation of exoticization, as harmless as it may initially seem. When a person is exoticized, s/he receives the message that s/he does not fall within what is defined as normative. This leaves one vulnerable to being reduced to an object or a spectacle and as such, the necessity to ask permission to touch the person is deemed nonessential or unimportant. Thus, a subtle message of inferiority is communicated; albeit unintentional, nonetheless, the message is still communicated and felt. This is integral to consciously or subconsciously viewing a person or a group as "the other," a concept explored by Homi K. Bhabha and other notable scholars like Frantz Fanon and Edward Said.[14] It is important for us to set these boundaries.

---

[14] Homi K. Bhabha, "The Other Question...Homi K Bhabha Reconsiders the Stereotype and Colonial Discourse," *University of Washington*, accessed March 20, 2012, http://courses.washington.edu/com597j/pdfs/bhabha_the%20othe r%20question.pdf.

If someone compliments your locks, gladly and graciously accept the compliment. If someone reaches for your hair and you feel uncomfortable, give yourself permission to unapologetically tell the person not to touch your hair and physically move away if necessary. You are in sole control over who can touch your hair or any other part of your body for that matter. Trust your intuition and permit yourself to set healthy boundaries.

Walking around with my locks falling past my shoulders, I am proud that my hair reflects a shared admiration I have for my African family around the globe. I reflect upon how the conscious decision to lock my hair was a decision to end my complicity with societal norms dictated by hatred and ignorance. The self-contempt I once possessed no longer has power over me. Pride in my beauty is pride in my people's beauty. And at the same time, I am painfully aware that my pride is inextricably bound to the shame, anger, and pain of my ancestors—the ancestors who cried worrisome tears for their children, the children who inherited a burden that was never theirs to carry. Everyday these locks allow me to stake a claim to the liberation that is rightfully theirs and mine. Let the ancestors stop weeping salty tears and celebrate that their descendants are coming home. *Ashe.*

Blackapina

First Movement: The Intersection

People of multiethnic backgrounds are accustomed to existing at the intersections of multiple worlds and multiple identities, holding and juggling those spaces in tension.[15] We become adept at navigating in and out and through numerous ethnoracial and ethnocultural contexts. The more one enters and exits these contexts, and the more one critically examines racial hierarchy and essentialism and their impact on the dynamics between racial groups, the more pronounced one's experience of multiraciality and multiethnicity becomes. An understanding of critical race theory coupled with the

---

[15] The term "multiethnic" is used to denote a person who is comprised of more than one ethnicity. Based on the work of sociologist G. Reginald Daniel, I use "multiethnic," as opposed to "multiracial," considering the notion that ethnicity includes the concepts of both race and culture. Daniel states, "Ethnicity generally refers to a segment or subset of a larger society whose members are thought by themselves and/or others to share a common culture (beliefs, ideals, values, meanings, customs, artifacts), which sets them off from other groups in the society. However, these individuals also share a common ancestry or origin (real or imagined)—and thus may have similar or common geno-phenotypical traits—that distinguish them from other members of society as well. In addition, they may more or less participate in shared activities in which that common origin and culture are significant ingredients. Considering that ethnic formation includes notions of both race and culture, it might seem more appropriate in this book to use the term multiethnic, rather than multiracial." See G. Reginald Daniel, *More Than Black?: Multiracial Identity and the New Racial Order* (Philadelphia: Temple University Press, 2002), xv.

experience of existing within the interstices of life—surviving and thriving in a world dominated by binary thought and then being inspired to rise above the surface "unfragmented"—are vital for multiethnic people who seek to live out the fullness of their humanity. It requires a creativity that is prompted by the mere existence of the intersection in the road, as well as the time taken to reflect upon the ramifications of that intersection.

As a Blackapina, a woman of African-American and Filipino-American descent, I regularly reflect upon how truly I am embracing both sides of my heritage and how well I am serving the populations on both sides of my bloodline. Existing in this in-between space of ethnicities and critically examining this intersectionality informs and strengthens my ability to recognize the complexities and nuances that characterize life's mosaic. We, as multiethnic people, have the potential to navigate this world of complexity and nuance. We have the potential to create unconventional solutions for the intersections of life and inspire deep, reflective transformation. Living in the intersection forces us to deal with the multiple paths that come together; if those paths never meet, if the crossroads don't exist, there is almost no reason, no opportunity for creative outcomes to arise.

So what does it mean to be at the crossroads? It means to stand at any intersection, any meeting of multiple paths, and ask the question: So what do I do now? It is to welcome transition.

Binary thinking would suggest selecting one of two paths. Perhaps a more nuanced way of thinking that informs the experience of many multiethnic people would suggest entertaining or exploring the possibility of taking multiple paths simultaneously. It means daring ourselves to believe that it is possible to walk multiple paths at the same time, embracing the transition, defying the conventional, the orthodox, the hegemonic and actively walking all of those paths—becoming a living, breathing mosaic. And as one bravely walks the multiple paths, one can clear the way, knocking down all obstacles that obstruct the flow of understanding, of compassion, of cooperation. This strengthens the ability of humanity to cocreate a world predicated on our capacity to remain in dialogue and allow our ideas to build upon each other as opposed to being combative in nature. Consequently, any collaboration amongst human beings should reflect this spirit of interdependence, manifesting in a force that brings healing wherever there is brokenness.[16]

Second Movement: Multiple Contexts

Having a Filipino-American mother and an African-American father, I juggled both of my ethnic backgrounds throughout my childhood and adolescence. Momma was from the *barangay* of Labangon in Cebu and left a clerical job to come to the United States—the country she considered the

---

[16] "The First Movement: The Intersection" was adapted from an introduction originally written in my article, "Barack Obama: Embracing Multiplicity—Being a Catalyst for Change" for *Race, Gender, and the Obama Phenomenon: Toward a More Perfect Union?*, a text co-edited by G. Reginald Daniel and Hettie Williams.

"land of milk and honey." Da'y (Daddy for short) was from Shreveport, LA and hopped freight trains to California—one of approximately six million African-Americans who fled the oppression of the South during what came to be known as the Great Migration.[17] My biracial experience began with the very basic influences of food and language, eating Momma's *biko* and *bijon* and Da'y's hoe cakes and hot cakes, hearing Da'y sound "country" and Momma speak Cebuano.

It was 1989 when Momma died and Da'y was put in a convalescent hospital; I was 15 years old. Three years later, Da'y died, and I officially became an orphan, continuing to juggle my dual heritage along with the meaning of life in the absence of parental love. I was tossed around from one social worker to the next, telling my story over and over again, becoming attached to no one. Though the most immediate lifelines to my history were gone, my sense of self was informed by the memories my parents left behind, the Filipino relatives I moved in with, the holidays spent with my African-American relatives, and close high school and college friends. In the public sphere—school, church, work, commerce, etc.—I learned what was acceptable and unacceptable according to Eurocentric standards. Though my family was from a poor, working class background, I quickly learned how to operate effectively within a social environment that was predominantly white, middle-class, and Christian-centered. While I received messages about how certain ways of speaking and behaving commanded respect from those who lay at the

---

[17] Isabel Wilkerson, *The Warmth of Other Sons: The Epic Story of America's Great Migration* (New York: Random House, 2010), 9.

intersection of these social categories, I had to also remain socially fluent within predominantly Filipino and African-American environments, as well.

Death. New family. New school. More death. These were my adolescent years. And out of all of this, I was trying to figure out who I was and what purpose I had. I was a fairly quiet and private person to begin with, but losing Momma and Da'y drove me into a deeper silence where lethargy coiled around my spirit, making hope seem hilarious. I always planned for the worst so I could be prepared for disappointment. I cried and cried until I had no tears left; it wasn't as though the pain stopped—a raw ache always lingered, but tears only brought me partial relief, and I was sick of crying. I developed a callousness toward life, promising myself I'd never get hurt again. Little did I know that when you shut off one emotion, you end up shutting off others; so as I became numb to pain, I became numb to joy and all my laughs were hollow.

When I was around people I could trust—people who knew how to be gentle with me, but also recognized my strengths and knew how much I hated pity—I was vibrant, playful, and vocal. Some of these angels were relatives like my cousin Alison Rodriguez on my Filipino side, her husband Martin, and their two children, JoAnna and Chris. Alison became a lifeline to my Filipino family and implicitly reminded me that indeed there was a time when Momma did exist. Martin became a symbol of what it meant to let go of the past as he embraced members of our family who initially didn't accept him because he was Mexican. Eventually, his family in Cuernavaca became my family and introduced a third culture into my upbringing. I felt a special connection to JoAnna and Chris partly because they were biracial like me. I assumed the responsibility of being the best *tia* I could be, which included nurturing their Mexipina(o) identity.

Most of the angels in my life were friends, teachers, and mentors—or a combination. In my adulthood, a period in life when I thought I wouldn't need parents, I found a new mother and father amidst this group of angels. It took me over 20 years before I was able to embrace new parents and not feel as though I was betraying my birth parents. Many adults struggle to express their new "grown-up" needs to parents who had always known them, but perhaps never completely understood or accepted them. I have somehow been spared this experience; instead, I am able to choose the new parents of my adulthood not only according to how well they suit my emotional and spiritual needs, but also based on how well we relate to one another. Today, I am blessed with their love and blessed with opportunities to share my love with them.

My new father, Tom Shepardson, is my former high school history teacher. He is white of Italian, English, Scottish, German, Austrian, Dutch and Native-American ancestry. His gentleness and patience have been priceless. Observing his comfort with being an introvert allowed me to accept my own introvert side. His ability to listen to me and affirm me throughout my adolescent and adult life is the reason why I believe I am a sane and loving person today. I consider Tom, his wife Diana, and their three children Katie, Anna, and Louis to be blood.

Vangie Canonizado Buell, a Filipino-African-American woman and mother to many (including three loving daughters of her own) has become my mom, auntie, confidant, mentor, and the *lola* to my daughter. We share a common ethnic mix and complex family history. This woman is an activist and a "connector," taking great pleasure in introducing good people to good people.[18] She is a patient, good listener, with a keen awareness about the various systems of oppression and privilege that exist in the United States. I can rest in her spirit and find inspiration there—a feeling I thought I'd never experience again.

Mama Vangie and Dad have never met, yet they have me in common. My new parents have been a constant source of support and guidance. Their warmth and wisdom have sustained and strengthened me. They've always believed in my integrity, generosity, intellect, and strength of character, and never doubted that my African-American and Filipino-American heritages were integral to my beauty as a human being.

Third Movement: The Blend

Being both African-American and Filipino-American means having the benefit of drawing from the richness of both ethnicities and bearing the responsibility of sharing both ethnicities with all I come in contact with. It means understanding and living out the complex interplay between

---

[18] Malcolm Gladwell, *The Tipping Point: How Little Things Can Make a Big Difference* (New York: Little, Brown & Company, 2000), 38-48.

culture, race, and ethnicity on a daily basis. Throughout my life, I was constantly searching for a word or label that would communicate my pride in both sides. Identifying as only African-American or Filipino-American never felt right because it just wasn't true. College and scholarship applications told me, "Please choose one," but categories like African-American and Asian/Pacific Islander felt too constraining. Friends, family, and strangers frequently asked me, "Are you more Filipino than Black or more Black than Filipino," questions that reflect a dangerous polarization and discomfort with nuance. Such binary thinking dictates how many of us operating in a Western context tend to approach people and ideas; we are conditioned to choose between or identify with one of two extremes—black and white, rich and poor, good and evil—suggesting that one couldn't possibly: 1) identify with more than one thing at the same time, 2) embrace a perspective or state of being somewhere in between, or 3) have multiple options to choose from other than the two presented.

Though such things were limiting, I never felt so frustrated by racial categories or questions reflecting binary thought that I longed to identify as "just human." This didn't fully capture what I was about either, especially since being both Black and Filipina shaped my human experience. My humanity was not something that could be extracted from its ethnic milieu. I was one who valued the unique histories of both sides and wanted to celebrate how being African-American and Filipina-American have shaped my human experience.

For many years I identified as half Black and half Filipino, figuring this was a way I could declare to the world that I was both.   However, identifying in terms of fractions reinforced a fragmented self-perception; it signified my silent insecurity about believing I was a diluted or counterfeit version of each ethnicity.   Since my Filipino features weren't immediately noticeable to most people in Lancaster, CA, I became aware that phenotypically I looked Black and therefore regularly reminded others that I was also Filipino, being sure to use the few Cebuano words I knew.   This was done partly to show pride in my Filipino side, but also to show myself off as not-your-average-Black-person—someone with an "interesting" twist.   I discovered that I received more attention when people learned I was mixed—not necessarily always good attention.   So as early as elementary school, long before I had the language for it, I had done what many had done to me: I exoticized myself.   I continued to do so until I became aware of some direct consequences of exoticization— not always feeling special and unique in a positive sense, but instead feeling freakish and less human.

During my late teens and early twenties, I noticed that I felt pressured to believe I had to turn on and off each side of my ethnic identity depending on who was around.   I thought that in order to be accepted as Black within an all Black social environment, I had to "turn on" my Black side (whatever that meant) and leave behind or downplay my Filipino side; when I was in an all Filipino environment I felt that I had to "turn on" my Filipino-ness (whatever that meant) and downplay my

Black side.[19] I felt like I was contextualizing; however, this wasn't satisfying and I continued to search for a way to contextualize without denying my other half. I wanted to *bring* all of me wherever I went, and I wanted all of me to be accepted regardless of whose company I was in.

Making attempts to be in touch with both sides, learning about the history of both and remaining socially connected to each community, I eventually became comfortable saying I was 100% African-American and 100% Filipino-American and devised various combinations of these terms. I was and am fully both. Identifying as such seemed to be a defiant response to the questions, "Are you more Filipino than Black? More Black than Filipino?" Not only was I proud to be both, but I was also proud to be a woman. So, beginning in my late twenties, I found ways to embrace my womanhood as I bounced between several ways of identifying: Filipino-African-American woman. African-Filipino-American woman. Filipina-African-American. African-Filipina-American. These names communicated the ideas of "together" and "distinct" at the same time.

Around this time, while working on my Master's thesis on precolonial West African and Filipino tricksters at San Francisco State University, I came across *Heirs of Prophecy*, a fantasy novel by Lisa Smedman, whose main character, Larajin, was half elf and half human. I was fascinated with how she invoked the deities from both her human and elven

---

[19] Since phenotypically I appear African-American to most people, it was a little more difficult to "turn off" my Black side than "turn off" my Filipino side.

sides. This caused me to stop thinking of being biracial as a deficit or an impurity. I began to wonder if instead I had the potential to be emotionally and spiritually stronger and more capable of facing life's challenges because I could call upon the assistance and guidance of deities on both sides of my ethnic heritage. From that point on, I've expanded the circle of deities that I address and thank during prayer, calling out to God, Eshu, Oshun, Yemaya, Bathala, Apolaki, Lakapati, and Diyan Masalanta. Consequently, I have learned more about the multidimensionality of the Divine, gaining greater clarity about the multiple ways the Divine manifests itself on Earth.

In early 2007, the possibility of identifying as "Blackapino" or "Blackapina" crossed my mind. The term floated around in my head for a bit, but didn't seem to get concretized for quite some time. I didn't have the courage to use it, but I couldn't completely articulate why. In retrospect, I know some of this had to do with my discomfort with blending terms, as if the process of blending would corrupt the ethnic essence of each side. This was an indication that I was still afraid of being viewed as a diluted version of a Filipina or African-American. I was also hesitant to use the term because to untutored ears it evoked only laughter and was never taken seriously; hidden in the laughter, I could almost hear people say, "Aw, that's cute and catchy. But is that real? Is that a real, lived experience?"

Folded into this transition were memories of a number of scholars who researched and published articles on multiracial identity. Such scholars either used blended terms or used concepts that involved blending. I remember the early writing of Rudy Guevarra, Jr. in which he explored the experiences of multiethnic people of Mexican and Filipino descent, becoming the first to use the term "Mexipinos" in a published work. [20]   From his clothing line, Multiracial Apparel, I bought some shirts for my niece and nephew that read, "Mexipino" and "Mexipina." [21] Shortly following the release of my memoir in 2005, I met Matthew M. Andrews, the first to conduct research focusing on multiracial identity specifically amongst those of both African-American and Filipino-American descent.[22]

A few years later, during the summer of 2007, I delivered a presentation at the Loving Decision Conference on precolonial West African and Filipino tricksters being empowering, decolonizing role models for biracial people of African-American and Filipino-American descent. There, I had the pleasure of listening to Rebecca Romo present her research about biracial people of African-American and Mexican-American descent and remember how freeing it was to hear her use the label "Blaxican."[23]   Susan Leksander

---

[20] Rudy P. Guevarra, Jr., "Burritos and *Bagoong*: Mexipinos and Multiethnic Identity in San Diego, California" in *Crossing Lines: Race and Mixed Race Across Geohistorical Divide*, ed. Marc Coronado, Rudy P. Guevarra, Jr., Jeffrey Moniz, and Laura Furlan Szanto (Santa Barbara: Multiethnic Student Outreach, University of California, Santa Barbara, 2003), 74.

[21] Guevarra recently released *Becoming Mexipino—Multiethnic Identities and Communities in San Diego*.

[22] Matthew M. Andrews, "(Re)Examining (Multi)Racial Identity: Black-Filipino Multiracials in the San Francisco-Bay Area" in *The Berkeley McNair Research Journal* (Berkeley: Trio, University of California, Berkeley, 2005), 27-38.

[23] Rebecca Romo, "Blaxican Identity: An Exploratory Study of Multiracial Blacks/Chicana/os in California" (presentation, National

presented research on applying the concept of psychosynthesis to multiracial clients. Leksander described psychosynthesis as a process within Western psychology that drew from various traditions including an African worldview describing how each human being is "seen as a community in and of itself, including a plurality of selves."[24] She pointed out the normalcy of each person having many subpersonalities and stated the following:

> Subpersonalities are thought to form in response to a "unifying center," a center of meaning that evokes a deep response in us. Different subpersonalities might arise in relationship to many different unifying centers—"parents, siblings, school, profession, philosophical systems, religious environments and the natural world."[25] I would add to this cultural and ethnic communities. A unifying center can be contacted at any age, from our earliest relationships to experiences late in life. What one experiences as outside of oneself, with enough exposure and meaning, eventually becomes internalized as a

---

Association for Chicana and Chicano Studies Annual Conference, San Jose, CA, April 1, 2008), 64.

[24] O.A. Ogbonnaya, "Person as Community: African Understanding of the Person as an Intrapsychic Community." *Journal of Black Psychology* 20(1)(1994), 75, quoted in Susan Leksander, "Psychosynthesis and Multiracial Clients: Diversity and Integration of Multiple Selves" (San Francisco: California Institute of Integral Studies, 2007), 2.

[25] J. Firma and A. Gila, *Psychosynthesis: A Psychology of the Spirit* (Albany: State University of New York Press, 2002), 73, Ibid., 12.

> subpersonality. This new identity internalizes and consolidates the skills, gifts, drives, qualities, beliefs and values activated and gained in response to the unifying center.[26]

Her research put my complex relationship with my African-American and Filipino-American backgrounds into perspective. At various times throughout my life, different aspects of each ethnicity seemed to be "outside" of myself since I had fashioned my life after the white dominant paradigm. In order to fully understand what it meant to live out my African-American and Filipino-American identity with depth and integrity, I consciously exposed myself to the people, language, arts, and history of each side to the point where each ethnicity gradually became internalized as one of my subpersonalities. My nucleus of subpersonalities was and will continue to be strengthened by my continuous immersion in social circles consisting of African-Americans, Filipino-Americans, women, introverts, extroverts, artists, athletes, theologians, healers, the various subgroups lying within each circle, and the intersection of all these and more. This nucleus is a tight, yet fluid, ever-expansive, ever-evolving blend housed within my spirit. I possess an authenticity that laughs in the face of essentialism. I am "Blackapina."[27] Black.

---

[26] Susan Leksander, "Psychosynthesis and Multiracial Clients: Diversity and Integration of Multiple Selves" (San Francisco: California Institute of Integral Studies, 2007), 12.

[27] The first Blackapino I met was Lance Adderly. Our mothers, Lucrecia Adderly and Lucrecia Stickmon, and our fathers, John Adderly and Fermon Stickmon, became friends in the 1970's and

Filipino-American. Woman.   I am an African-American unafraid of identifying as Black because it hearkens back to the Black Power Movement when Black, the color and the culture, were embraced with pride. I also use it because *bibi*, the word for "black" amongst the Sonay of Mali, referred only to "the essential goodness of things"—a definition predating the distortion and demonization of the color.[28]   I am a second-generation Filipina-American, holding my mother's immigrant dreams and sacrifices; as my *utang na loob*, I offer Momma the fruits of my work as professor of Filipina(o)-American Heritage and Africana Studies. I am a woman who menstruates and gives birth and nurses and nurtures and fights. I am each of these and more. I am all these at the same time. I live at the crossroads, straddling multiple worlds.

---

consequently we became childhood playmates. Thanks to his mother, he and I were recently reunited. It is only in my adulthood that I understand how those early years of playing together prevented me from feeling like the lone Blackapino in the world. Since 2004, I began meeting other multiracial people of African-American and Filipino-American descent like Vangie Canonizado Buell, Tony Robles, Matthew M. Andrews, Dennis Calloway, and Teresa Hodges. Thanks to the work of Myrna and Carlos Zialcita, I learned about jazz artists who were also Black and Filipino like Sugar Pie DeSanto, Bob Porlocha, Elizabeth Ramsey, Joe Bataan, Lena Sunday, and Anna Maria Flechero. In 2011, I learned that long before I identified as Blackapina, Joe Bataan used a blended term, "Afro-Filipino" to describe himself. Bataan released an album in 1975 called *Afro-Filipino* which included a song entitled, "Ordinary Guy (Afro-Filipino)."

[28] Wade Nobles, *Seeking the Sakhu: Foundational Writings for an African Psychology* (Chicago: Third World Press, 2006), 329.

Hybridity is my home where transition and nuance are always welcome. At the interstices, you'll hear my breath. When I walk, listen for the sound of ancestral spirits and deities hailing from the African continent and the Philippine Islands; hear them pulse and drift, cry and whisper, laugh and pray as they clear the way for their children to walk the world protected, guided, and strengthened. *Ashe.*

(FOR:) PLAY—An Exegesis of Goapele's "Play"

Consider it a precious gift when a woman tells her lover she is ready to play. In all its vulnerability, strength, and beauty, her Love must be recognized as sacred and held gently. In the reality of the moment, the lover should understand the weight behind the softness in her eye and the longing in her voice—yes, she's serious. When she initiates, the lover must seize the opportunity and trust in the exciting potential of the surreal, exploratory world she wants to lead him to. Her Love finds its root in the spirit realm and in the depth and integrity of her emotional self. She is fully aware that her Love cannot be coaxed from her. She cannot be coerced into loving. She must give it freely—only then will it be genuine and whole.

Goapele's latest single, "Play," captures this profound union of the sacred and the sexy with the perfect marriage between a sensuous, dreamlike voice, snapping fingers, and the deep bass sounds reminiscent of heartbeats.[29] Opening with the soft growl of a lion, "Play" is for the woman who knows what she wants and isn't afraid to say so. "Play" is for the woman turned on by everything from the pulsing, hypnotic beats of Art of Noise in "Moments in Love" to the funky, nasty vibe of Ginuwine's "Pony." It's for the woman who is enticed by Floetry's "Say Yes" and Alicia Keys' "Unthinkable." It's for the woman in the club, dancing to "Ill Na Na" by Foxy Brown and Jay Z, feeling sexy and powerful

---

[29] Goapele, "Play," in *Break of Dawn* (Oakland: Skyblaze Recordings, 2011), MP3.

for a brief moment, only to feel empty seconds later. And most importantly, "Play" is for the woman turned on by leading—leading her lover to a magical, spiritual world that has no rules...and for the man who has no problem following.

Goapele takes the listener for an erotic ride that soothes and arouses in a single breath. She begins by getting a sense of where her lover's thoughts lie, singing, "I wanna know what you wanna do. What if I could say there wasn't any rules? I wanna play, play around." No time is wasted—the desire to know what her lover is thinking reveals itself as a sexual invitation. By the time we hear the second line, she makes it clear that she wants to play and dangles the idea of infinite possibilities. All the lover knows is that this world is boundless and yet she sings, "Tell me if you think that you can get down!" Her lover is given a playful challenge to enter into this world of play—a world that has gone undefined, and thus all the more seductive.

The world is set in motion as we enter the refrain, and she tells her lover, "Come here baby I'm ready to touch you. Listen to me, nothing's too much, when I'm ready to play...Come here let me whisper in your ear. Tell you how I'm about to make you feel. I'm ready to play, we could play this game all day." As she whispers in her lover's ear, our imaginations fill in the gap, allowing us to envision what she has in mind—all the things that would satiate her desire; all the things that would make her lover call out her name. From the whisper to the nameless game, Goapele's words are provocative and filled with innuendo. Not only does this suggestive language draw in the lover (and the listener), it also renders Woman as sexually healthy, not hypersexualized; she is in full control of her body and intent. In a single verse, Goapele gracefully counters the image of the silent, passive woman relegated to disposable sex toy, while at the same time dodges potential critics eager to castigate a woman for being dirty and unladylike just because she is explicit. In the whisper, she could be explicit or subtle. We'd never know. The beauty is that she remains a woman—complete and whole—regardless.

In the second verse, Goapele sings, "I wanna go where you've never been, and this not me trying to give in. Said you had a taste, but you really don't know. I think I can help what you're looking for." She points out, "...this is not me trying to give in," being aware of the difference between choosing to act and being forced to act. She's not leading him to this world of play because she feels pressured. Instead, this desire is born from her own will. The woman is wholeheartedly leading the way to this place that is new to the lover. He's only had a "taste," but she possesses the fullness of Truth. She knows the epitome of exploratory play and ecstasy. It is so rich, so full that by the end of the song, she promises, "You'll feel it all in your soul." This world of sexual play transcends the trappings of the flesh to the point where he will feel it in the very core of his being. Through this experience, she offers a glimpse of the Divine.

This offering of the spirit realm is evident throughout the rest of the second verse in Goapele's lyrics, as well as in the music of her producers Electric Thunderbolt, Teddy Thunderbolt, and Dan Electric. When comparing the second verse to the first, we see a couple of subtle, yet profound changes.   In contrast to the first verse where she says, "'Cause this is what I'm dying for. I mean this is what I'm dying to do," we find that in the second verse she sings, "'Cause this is what we're living for. I mean this is what we're dying to do." Goapele switches from "I" to "we" as if to suggest that he has already accepted the invitation and a union has taken place. This desire to play is not hers alone, but is a joint desire now. We also see what was once an experience that she is "dying for" and "dying to do" has transformed into both "what we're living for" and "what we're dying for." Meanwhile, her lyrics are enhanced by sounds of the sky opening up and sunshowers falling to the Earth—sounds almost identical to what we hear when she sings, "You'll feel it all in your soul."

When one is living for something, there's nothing else she'd rather do. Her dreams and fantasies have been fulfilled. When one is dying to do something, he can't wait for his dreams and fantasies to come true; the dream/fantasy has yet to unfold. The ethereal sounds of sunshowers coupled with the paradox of both living and dying describe the height of sexual experiences—the place where the boundary between this world and the spirit realm is blurred; where we lie on the cusp of night and day; where speed is just as meaningful as being slow and steady; where the nasty and the sweet share a border that gets crossed daily.

Goapele's "Play" is particularly striking because a woman is initiating sexual foreplay. Although we live in an age where perhaps it is more acceptable (compared to decades ago) for women, within a heterosexual context, to "make the first move," men are still, for the most part, socially conditioned to be the one to initiate romance and/or sex. At the same time, women, in the name of modesty and decency, are taught to play hard to get and to eventually give in to a man's pursuit, believing that his persistence is a sign of his true love. As a result, she receives the message that it is acceptable, if not preferable, to become overwhelmed by a man's advance *and then* give her love in return. According to those who may consider themselves traditional, the act of a woman initiating a sexual advance is perceived as putting her at risk of losing the man since her "directness" may cause him to feel emasculated. This song subtly challenges that paradigm. The woman, of her own volition, knows that she is ready and invites her lover to a place he's never been. With broad strokes, she paints an image of this world of play, setting no limits. The key is that the woman is leading. She doesn't need instructions. She has the instruction manual. In fact, she wrote it. And guess what? It is fluid and filled with the potential for exploration and excitement. When a woman's sexual desire is born from her own will, she is fully invested and her sexual gratification becomes central. The only questions that remain are: "Does she say how she wants her lover to make her feel? Can he keep up? Is she satisfied?" Perhaps, answers lie in the whisper. Perhaps, in another song. Or maybe the next play session. Time will tell. *Break of Dawn* drops this Monday, October 24, 2011.

Birthmark

nickel-sized mole
near top of my inner thigh
along bikini line
cursed you my whole life

throughout childhood
adolescence
wished you were never there
kept you hidden
never shown to one soul
bathtub & shower curtain
have only seen you

didn't want unwanted eyes
staring at my crotch
never talked about you
didn't want unwanted minds
thinking about you
mark of shame
picturing you
fantasizing about you
dark black
nickel-sized mole

scared to have you
mistaken for pubic hair
covered you at the pool
pulled down my swimsuit

over you
wore men's swim trunks
so no worry
about you showing up

thought about putting you
out of your misery
removing you

Dr. Hammond
always told Momma

"Be careful. Keep an eye on it. If it gets bigger or if hair
grows from it, have it checked. It might be cancerous. You
know you could always freeze it off. That's easy!"

easy
easy
never did it
too scared
too scared to have it removed
removal traded for
lifetime of birthmark limbo
forty years with you
and you're still there
why did I keep you

my latent hope that
one day I'd get used to you

or maybe love you?

&

strong and healthy
waiting to be seen
to make her guest appearance
her grand entrance

forty now
and what's sexy

birthmark
dark black
sexy you
nickel-sized
black sexy

ready now
to show you off

red bikini
gold hooks at bosom
cowry shells on straps
bikini bottom ties
bikini wax
smooth
let the world see
see me

invoke Naomi & Kimora
and walk

own it
swing enough to know what's mine
and give 'em back the rest

let's see what happens

fuck inhibitions
they've done me no good

Sexy

slip on them black stockings
snap them garters
wrap me in cold satin
i wanna feel this with every step
loving what's within

self-love
waking me in the night
easing my fantasies
of what the next day
holds

excitement
uncontained
this orgasm
never leaves me lonely

confidence inviting people in
holding their eyes with mine
and their eyes holding me

my soul can't hold in this light
manifesting in the flow of my arms
the switch of my hips
the caress of my palms
released in the pound of my tenor swing

when I speak

i relax
spread out
shoulders roll and pulse
with the sudden sound
found only
in the interruptions of life
the accidents of life

my rhythm slows you down
match my speed

when I speak
you want to look for me
find me
and touch the soft edge
you hear

then I speak with smiles and winks
and say
come visit me
be with me
ride my wave
tremble with me

but in the same breath
the same wink and smile
i say I'm bound to no object of desire

making me dangerous
as I draw

anyone
everyone
in

my body
a rip curl
splashing
turquoise
emerald
burgundy
indigo

my body
flexible
bottom or top

it gives
it takes
it's tough
it's gentle
it's pure
it fights
it rests
it flexes
it sweats
it's wet
it squirts
it's dirty

quiet command of surroundings

not bossy

smooth stroke
clear core
certitude
rolls off spirit
melting hearts
so shame
forgets its own name

Here's the Truth

No, I don't want to swallow your cum!
How the fuck is that sexy?!!

I want…

I want… malted mocha body paint, some canela, vanilla in there.
I don't want whipped cream and strawberries…too generic…
Give me raspberries—they're soft and wet like me.
Spread that paint with your fingers against my every bend and curve.
Please start at my neck.
From there, I don't care. Move wherever you'd like.

Peel me,
Let the juice drip off the side.
Bring me where you are,
                where your spirit lies,
                        where your fear dies.
Where intention meets accident,
Bring me there.

Don't forget a raspberry for each nipple—a reminder to never pinch or
twist.
Turn me over and paint strokes of chocolate down my spine.
Lay a trail of raspberries on top, from the base of my neck to the flesh of
my hips.
Lick and eat, slow and sweet, leaving behind gentle kisses and…and…
I'll wipe the chocolate from your lips and place it on mine to save it for
later…

Hear my breath, don't time it, don't explain it.
Just hear it and let it be. Know that it is mine and I freely share it with you.

I was awakened, alarmed by the question, "Whose pussy is this?"
I'd always say "Yours."
This time I said, "This pussy is mine!"
He left.
I smiled.
I haven't compromised.
I still want my raspberries.

Leave Tomorrow

(Dedicated to women who need to go in order to live.)

not sure
if you'll see me
momma
yemaya
diyan masalanta
see me
anytime soon

maybe next time
maybe
please stay
are you there
la virgen de guadalupe
tonantzin
mother mary
lakapati
mawu
maybe next time…

His love doesn't always feel like love…I know
His love makes you cry
His love, his sex—your tears, your vomit.
You scrub and scrub
His semen cemented to your body and memory
Wipe and wipe
His kisses remain
You thought you'd get used to it

You hoped things would get better…until they didn't

Anak
Mija

How long have you let his hatred dictate your destiny?
How long have you lost hope that love truly exists?
How many times did he fail to see how precious you are?
How many sorries does it take to win your forgiveness?

Your heart is priceless

I know your faith in him has run out,
But you still have faith in yourself

If he wiped the poison from his eyes he could see
That you are the saffron rose you smell everyday
The flowers, the vines, the trees, they are your kin
And he'd feel at home in your forest
And place lilacs in your hair

Sit with you
And listen to your song
Massage your feet
Stroke your arms
And ask
So how are you
        so how are you
                how are you feeling
                        what's on your mind

so how are you

And when you stop to look at the Earth,
                he'll ask you what you see
                        he'll ask you what you see
                                he'll ask you what you see
To see through your eyes
All that he missed

If he only knew how precious you are
If only he noticed you
If only he noticed you
He'd know your value
And treat you as though you're worth being loved

Because he knows you won't wait forever
Because he knows you could leave tomorrow
The second he stops noticing
Because he knows you could leave tomorrow

You can leave tomorrow

It's okay
Always remember you can leave tomorrow
And I would take care of you
I promise
                I promise   do you hear me?   I promise

You are here today
But *if* you change your mind

But *if* you change your mind
When you change your mind
If you need to change your mind
I will be there

Don't violate the very core of yourself by staying
Waiting for "it won't ever happen again"
To happen again

With bruises on your face
And bruises on your heart,
I weep for you
I reach for you

Where are you?
Where were you?

You were so close,
        but you did not come.

I called for you
I call for you

You did not come
You're not coming

Where did you go?

Come with me now
It is clear

Come with me now

My daughters,
Why have sex with a man who doesn't know your spirit
My daughters
How many times will you believe him
When he says his penis will break your fever

My daughters
How many more times will you be violated

because he
thinks
you're the
cure for
AIDS

My daughters
How many times
How many times
Will you die inside

My God

Run, my babies, run   love doesn't look
like this

                you're not meant for this

Your love cannot be coaxed from you

Cannot be won by forced kisses and a million spoken "I love
you's"

We freely give our Love daily
That's how it works
We give our Love to whomever we please
Our Love: many forms, many layers given away

And daughters, since your beauty is so pure,
A true love will be in awe of your every thought
Your every feeling
Tickled by your quirks
Comforted by your gentleness, your simplicity, your
complexity

Believe me when I say
You are not worthless
You deserve to be treated like the flowers in your hair
                    Shown off
                Praised for the life you bring

A true love who knows this
Will believe this
And will remember you could always leave tomorrow

Love Musings

Musing 1

As I relearn what love means and feel the tug and pull between "love as discipline" and "the falling in love" feeling, I find that my knowledge of love is becoming more refined.[30]   One thing I can say is that it is a distressing feeling to wait to see if my love for Sterling will grow. I find it deeply unkind to give love time constraints and then tell it to grow. And yet that is precisely what I have done. Not sure what it will develop into.

Musing 2

There really is something about the small and large decisions we make and how they inadvertently cause us to cross paths with an incredible person.   It's those interruptions...those times we change our minds...those accidents...that set beautiful things into motion. And we have no idea what kind of symphony lies before us. Life is beautiful!

Musing 3

No matter what we as human beings perceive as our weaknesses, shortcomings, etc., the Divine knows us so well that s/he lovingly embraces those shortcomings and still allows things to happen for us so we may know love. I think we are regularly presented with opportunities to know what love (what God) looks like through our human relationships.

---

[30] A concept explored by M. Scott Peck in *The Road Less Travelled*.

Musing 4

I think it is hard when a woman or a man makes it their life's mission to be generous, open, and tender...wanting to bring just enough sunshine into people's lives to remind them that they matter. For those who have managed with very little light or perhaps the wrong type of light, such people's actions can be misinterpreted. That's the mistake I made when I fell in love with Larkin. I've been trying to get him out of my system ever since. Measured every man against him—the Larkin Index. It hasn't been fair for every man I've ever loved, including Sterling. Next time, I need to ask myself if I will accept a man for not being Larkin.

Musing 5

More on love...I have been thinking of the question of the "falling in love" feeling versus "love as discipline" and whether these two can coexist. Forgive me if this sounds too grandiose, but perhaps the purpose of the "falling in love" feeling is to give people a glimpse of how it feels...somewhat of an incentive to ensure that we will put in some effort to maintain that love. This reminds me of how you likened commitment in a relationship to the cultivation of a garden. How it's that type of maintenance that allows a relationship to grow. For example, when the love seems to get old or feel absent, a couple must do something to stay curious about each other, fascinated with each other...so they may never lose track of the changes, the growth the other experiences.

Musing 6

I think I will always believe in the magic that is felt when two people fall in love...the glimmer in the eye; the feeling that you've met this person before when you've only known her/him for 10 minutes. I love it because I can't control it. Because it surprises me. I'm a lover of wonder. I just have to make sure that I have more love for the person than for the "falling in love" feeling.

Musing 7

On a different note, after talking to a friend about the subject of "love as discipline," she introduced something else into my vocabulary: dissociation. That sometimes when we think we are being disciplined about staying in a relationship, we may actually be distancing ourselves from a problem because it's too much to bear...dissociating ourselves from the problem, minimizing it in the relationship, denying the issue is there, convincing ourselves that everything is okay...all for the purpose of being able to cope. She said that indeed there will be some ups and downs and that being committed of course requires work...but then she ended with something that hit me: "Love isn't supposed to be hard."

Musing 8

I think after continuously being in each other's presence, it is possible for one or both to all of a sudden notice something about the other that "turns them on" or makes their heart melt: the way he strokes his hair; the scent of his cologne; the gentleness of his touch; the tenderness of his words; the sun shining in her eyes, revealing a shade of brown he never noticed before; the way she stops to pick up a leaf and sees a drop of water on it; how she calls out his shit with a tone that no one else dares to use with him; how she smells a rose. Or embarrassing moments like: when he trips on a crack in the sidewalk; when his glasses fog up after opening the dishwasher; when her ice cream falls on the ground; when she bumps into a pole; when she dips her shrimp tempura in her tea instead of the sauce. I think all these can open the door to the "falling in love" feeling.

Musing 9

Long-term commitments professing to last forever underestimate the meaning of forever. We don't always take into consideration the kinds of changes a person goes through in one lifetime. When you fall in love with a person, you fall in love with who they are in the moment; their qualities meet your heart's standards of attraction *in that moment*. But what if your standards change? And what if the person changes. Truly if you profess to stay with someone forever, you are vowing to love what they will become—having faith that what they will become will still resonate with what you will become. But you really don't know if that will happen.

Response to a Fellow Introvert

...The introvert and the ground seem to have a lot in common. Same energy. Same pace perhaps. I came across something by Luisah Teish that talked about the West African perspective on life in all things and she spoke of rock having the energy of being (and animals have the energy of doing; humans have the energy of self-reflective consciousness, etc.).[31] It reminds me that the Earth has its rhythm, too.

Some words/concepts that have stayed with me for the past six years or so have been: Steady. Anchor. Safety net. Still water. In some way or another, these things remind me of depth, home, stability, and stillness...ultimately suggesting what it means to be present and rooted.

Yeah, you're talking to a fellow introvert. Not sure if this is something you could already detect or if this is surprising. I'm much more extroverted now than just a few years ago. Accepting myself as such has been a challenge given how society in the U.S. tends to favor the extrovert. For most of my life, I have been painfully shy...only being extroverted with those I felt most comfortable with. I consider myself (like my Dad, Tom) to be an introvert with extrovert skills. It is because of him that I learned how to fully accept myself as an introvert. The extrovert skills I do have mostly developed because of teaching. However, I am most at home with my

---

[31] Luisah Teish, *Jambalaya* (San Francisco: HarperCollins, 1985), 62.

introvert side.

For me, what grounds me is feeling or observing moss on rock, watching a fern bounce in the breeze and listening to the rhythm of the ocean's current. I think out of all these, the moss understands me the most.

Accident

On my way to work, driving down Highway 29, I was rear-ended by some car that felt big and fast. I was wondering when the impact would end and how much further my car would be pushed along the highway. That big, fast car created a chaos in me that left me shaking with no time to picture myself in my own future. It was a sudden future, tragically and magically still. I got out of the car and looked at it.

It was an accordion. The trunk was in the back seat. Windows shattered. Didn't bother to look at the front, having no idea I was pushed into another car. When I picked up the police report, I discovered I was in a four-car accident. I was the first to be rear-ended. I never did see the faces of the drivers of the two cars in front of me. But I know we were all affected. We were forever bound by that moment, all because the driver of that Black Lexus SUV felt a drop of water fall from her sky roof onto her head. And she looked up.

I looked at my car. Looked at the driver standing behind it. Looked at my car again.

"Oh my God, Oh my God. Thank God my baby wasn't in the car. Thank God my baby wasn't in the car," was all I could say.

The woman admitted fault right on the spot.

"I'm sorry, I'm sorry. I have kids, too. I have kids, too. I'm sorry," she said, virtually on the verge of tears, not knowing what to do with her hands, as she covered her mouth, put them on her head, crossed her arms. I knew what to do with my hands. That's why I didn't get too close to her.

I was rushed to the emergency room at Kaiser Vallejo. I was at the mercy of two strangers in the Piner ambulance. Thank God for kind strangers who know precisely what to say, what to ask. Through touch and word, they reassured me that indeed I was a human being and still alive and worthy of attention and gentleness.

Within a few hours, I was released from the hospital with no more than whiplash and some back pain. No bruises, no blood, no scratches.

⁊

Nothing was more comforting than dicing carrots. That was one of many tasks involved in preparing my daughter's lunch each day. Such routines save our lives. Grocery shopping, going to work, sending emails, making phone calls, washing dishes, doing laundry, and paying bills are the hamster wheels that distract us from the lofty concepts of life, love, death and God. They help us develop a certain callousness to the profundity of life so we are not constantly reminded of how fragile and finite our human existence is. Hamster wheels can keep us from reaching our fullest potential, but they can also save us from the enormous task of pondering the ontological on a daily basis to the point where we find ourselves analyzing the hell out of a milkshake as opposed to simply enjoying it. They can also be infused with meaning and joy depending on the degree to which we take care of the real human beings with the real human spirits who are involved in and/or impacted by tasks that seem inconsequential. They create the illusion that tomorrow is promised. And like hamsters, we go about our business because, for the moment, such things bring us a satisfaction that we don't know is only temporary. As human beings, we cannot handle thinking about the reality of our mortality every single day. Otherwise, we might explode; or at least that's a looming fear. The moment our routines are interrupted by car accidents, violence, war, or other trauma-inducing events that cause us to face our mortality, we experience a sense of surprise or awakening when such things happen. It's like someone coming around the corner, handing you a note saying, "Guess what? You're human. You might die today." And this comes from the privileged perspective of a person who lives in relative peace and stability. I can only imagine how this insight might change if I lived in a war-torn country or in a neighborhood right here in the United States where people are at war with each other and with systems of oppression. Only my fellow sisters and brothers who live in such constant turmoil could share how they experience their mortality.

Every time someone close to me dies, I am reminded of my mortality. And in the accident, I was reminded of that mortality…even though I was spared. Or maybe because I was spared, I am once again prompted to think about my breath and vision being temporal. Why *am* I alive? What does this mean? Should I cherish this day? Should I do more good deeds? Or is it more than good deeds? Should I believe in justice? Does this mean I should be afraid and stay afraid? Yes. Yes to all of it. I guess.

Be afraid.

Love like you've never loved before.

Celebrate like you've never celebrated before.

Why? Because you were spared. I was spared. Who was protecting me? By not being in the car, my daughter was spared...my husband was spared. Who was protecting them? Who was protecting us? And why?

What kind of work do God and the ancestors want me to do? Have I left a deep enough impression on the world? Do I stay in relationships that I deserve to be in? Or do I hold onto relationships because I feel like I have no other choice? Is it possible to create choices in what feels like a vacuum chamber? To do so seems to be the equivalent of stepping forth and declaring myself a magician. Maybe that's what I'm supposed to do at times: create magic. Or maybe just pay attention to the magic that's already there. Pay attention to God's grace as if that grace were twigs floating in a gutter just waiting to be picked up. And maybe...maybe I need to respond to that grace and start picking up those twigs.

I don't think we can answer these questions every single day of our lives. Correction. Perhaps we should be answering these questions everyday. Then maybe we'd live our lives a little differently. Live our lives as if we deserved love...all the while eating chips and cupcakes so we'll stop taking ourselves so seriously.

Magical

Facebook Post
December 21, 2011

My daughter has a book called *The Path that Allah Made*, and it talks about the gifts that lie ahead when one chooses to make *du'a* instead of taking the safe, set path that would surely bring you home.[32] *Du'a* (prayer) is a profound act of worship.[33] *Du'a* means "calling" in Arabic and refers to the "act of remembering" and calling upon Allah.[34] I am reminded once again that even by following an unexpected path we are welcoming the Divine to enter our lives. This is certainly what happened to me today. After my walk around the Petrified Forest, I entered the gift shop and didn't set out to "summon" or "invoke" the Divine…I was just having a brief, casual conversation with Alan, a man who works in the Petrified Forest gift shop. He said if I enjoyed the Petrified Forest, I should go to the Armstrong Redwoods about 40 minutes away. He described it as magical. So that's what I decided to do. The drive was gorgeous. A beautiful winery against a backdrop of redwood trees—a nice prelude to

---

[32] Adeeba Jafri, *The Path That Allah Made* (New Delhi: Goodword Books, 2003), 3.

[33] This line appears in the original post. However, the line that follows was added after December 21, 2011 to clarify the concept of du'a.

[34] "The Power of Du'a," *Shaykh Islam*, accessed June 28, 2012, http://www.islam786.org/powerofdua.htm#92435509.

entering the forest. The forest itself is incredible. A number of different hiking paths. Trees were enormous. Absolutely breathtaking and overwhelmingly beautiful. It felt like I was in Lothlorien. It was one of the few times that I found something so beautiful that I had to leave. Quite a strange feeling. Ordinarily, I want to stay in such places forever. Anyways, if you haven't already been here, you have to go! It's near Guerneville about 2 hours away from the East Bay.

A Perfect Ordinary Day

Preface

While writing "Beauty Revealed—Bringing Out the Best in Others," (the final selection in this book) I began jotting down notes focused on how to avoid stagnancy in order to stay motivated in life. Upon completing "Beauty Revealed," I realized I needed to flesh out the meaning of taking care of oneself. After introducing the concept of "choosing to live" in that article, the possibility of having a separate piece that married the concepts of self-care, "choosing to live," and avoiding stagnancy emerged. Consequently, "A Perfect Ordinary Day" was born.[35]

"A Perfect Ordinary Day" is based on my personal experience of taking care of myself for my own sake, as well as for the sake of those I love. A combination of philosophies and activities that are integral to my daily routine are shared in this essay. Activities that I practice less often— things I would benefit from if I practiced them more regularly—are also included.

This essay is written from the perspective of a mother, wife, writer, and humanities professor who relies daily on the power of the Divine. I am not speaking from the perspective of a certified physical trainer or a professional nutritionist. If your daily routine does not look like the schedule I have outlined below, I do not recommend beating

---

[35] "Beauty Revealed" follows "A Perfect Ordinary Day" in this text to reflect the significance and the necessity of taking care of oneself before one can be capable of caring for others.

yourself up about it; doing so would not, of course, constitute what I would call self-care. Part of caring for ourselves involves being patient and rejoicing in any progress we have made.

I encourage you to draw from your own research and personal experience when deciding how to best meet your individual emotional, physical, and spiritual needs. As you read "A Perfect Ordinary Day," please remember that you have the freedom to accept, trash, rework, and/or augment these practices and philosophies. You have the power to decide what to integrate into your daily life.

Introduction: Choosing to Live

I am breathing. I have a pulse. I exist.
I am grateful for another day.
But I want to do more than just exist?
I want to feel alive.

Feeling alive requires keeping a single mantra in mind: fulfill the heart's desires. We need to do all the things that make our eyes light up and inspire us to sing—the things that fill us with such passion and excitement that we can't wait to wake up in the morning. We need to make the conscious decision to live. *Choosing to live* means being open to receiving all the good the world has to offer. In the process, we must make sure we experience this openness to the world both in solitude and in the company of close friends and family.

When we *choose to live*, we have no option to be amongst the spiritually dead who condemn themselves to a lifetime of hopelessness. We can't maintain such an attitude just because the world told us that there's nothing out there but a life of pain. The moment we *choose to live*, we begin to behave in ways that are more loving toward ourselves and others: our imagination is liberated, and we can envision a multitude of possibilities that can bring people together in the spirit of mutual respect and understanding. We become more aware of the responsibility attached to living an emotionally, spiritually, and physically healthy lifestyle. We realize how crucial it is to take care of ourselves, for our own sake, as well as, for the sake of others. All the people we care for and spend time with—our families, friends, students, patients, and clients—rely on us for knowledge, wisdom, and nurturance. The more people we are responsible for in our daily lives, the greater is our responsibility to take good care of ourselves.

So how do we take care of ourselves? One simple answer: eat. We must eat "food" that nourishes our bodies, minds, and spirits. By "food," I don't mean just the food we ingest. I'm talking about emotional food—emotional nourishment.[36]

You can gain a sense of what this emotional food needs to be by first loving yourself. Accept and love everything that makes you You: your physical appearance; the

---

[36] Maintaining a healthy diet is not only important, but essential. Eating nutritious food and exercising regularly are among the many factors that can contribute to emotional wellness.

way you speak, think, walk, and laugh; your idiosyncrasies; your flaws; your likes; your dislikes.

There is a mysterious connection between accepting yourself in the "here and now" and feeling free to change. Some believe that in order to transform and grow all you need is the will to change and the knowledge of the essential steps that can make the desired change happen. This is true, but only partly true. One must also consider what ingredients are needed to ignite the will. One of those ingredients is full acceptance of the self. You must fully accept what already resides in your heart and soul, creating a stillness, a silence that steadies your spirit. In the way that efficiency requires regular breaks, staying energized and motivated requires time spent in stillness. Sometimes, you need to hold and caress your own spirit to keep it from quivering with worry, insecurity, blame, and regret. All too many of us wander the Earth preoccupied with the anxiety these things generate. Steady your spirit with self-acceptance and the belief that you are worth being loved and treated justly.

Pay close attention to what turns you on.
Ask yourself the questions:
What do I value? What do I like?

Once you come up with your answers, begin feeding yourself—begin nourishing yourself. Listen to music, watch films, and read books that you love. Look at photography and paintings that inspire the best and healthiest images to rest in your mind—images that keep you optimistic about the world's possibilities. Stay physically active so you can be in tune with your body and stay energized. Pray, meditate, and pay homage to the ancestors and the Creator. Sit with the Divine; see and respect how the Divine manifests herself/himself in human beings and in nature.

If we don't feed ourselves, we'll be spiritually empty. And if we're empty for too long, this emptiness can develop into starvation. Our starvation has devastating effects on the people we love. If we're not careful, we can kill our loved ones with our starvation—without even knowing it.

Starvation and Stagnancy

Starvation can be easily recognized in a person who feels stuck, unmotivated, always angry or sad, constantly pessimistic, and/or chronically indecisive for long periods of time; it could be months; it could be years. It's a state of stagnancy.

If we examine its origins, we find that the word "stagnancy" is derived from "stagnate," meaning "to cease to flow."[37] "Stagnate" comes from the Latin *stagnatus*, the past participle of *stagnare* which means "to cause to stand."[38] The prefixes *sta-* and *st(h)a-* trace their roots to an Indo-European base meaning "to stand."[39] We see this prefix obviously in

---

[37] Ernest Klein, *Klein's Comprehensive Etymological Dictionary of the English Language* (New York: Elsevier Scientific Publishing Company, 1971), 711.

[38] In Latin, *stagnare*, (to cause to stand) comes from *stagnum* meaning 'pool.' Ibid.

[39] Ibid., 712-713.

the word "stand," as well as in other words like "stasis," "stale," and "static."[40]

If we are just standing in one place, indeed we can soak in our surroundings, but we can't stay there forever; we have to move in order to carry out our daily activities. When water is stagnant, it becomes a breeding ground for bacteria and parasites. When bread is stale, it tastes dry and stiff and isn't so appetizing. If something is static, it stays put and doesn't move. Feeling stagnant is a lot like lying in a hospital bed, looking out the window, and watching people run, laugh, and play without you.

Though these analogies offer some insight into how I define stagnancy, I think it is important to further clarify what stagnancy is and what it isn't. First, avoiding stagnancy is not the same as staying busy. Staying busy with routines and/or meaningless activities can lead to burnout—and guess what: you're stuck again! Secondly, avoiding stagnancy is not the same as avoiding stillness. I view stagnancy as a more long-term, crippling state of being which can eventually control you; stillness—either literally being still or simply slowing down one's pace—is, on one hand, a more temporary state involving solitude and silence which can steady the spirit (as

---

[40] The verb, "to stand" comes from Middle English *standen* which comes from Old English *standan*. It also has an influence from the Latin *stare* meaning "to stand" which finds its root in the Indo-European base (as mentioned above) *st(h)a-* meaning "to stand." "Stasis" and "static" have a combination of Latin and Greek influences which trace their origin to the Indo-European base (as mentioned above) *sta-* meaning "to stand." "Stale" meaning "not fresh or stagnant" is from the Middle English *stale* meaning "that which has stood long." See Ibid., 711-713.

mentioned earlier); stillness is something you can choose; it's a time for reflection and respite; it allows you to be present to yourself and to the universe. Taking time to be still can enable you to make clear, sound decisions in the future.

On the other hand, while the act of entering into stillness and staying there for a moment is temporary, there is also a way that stillness finds a permanent home within you. With practice, I believe stillness can be embedded into your spirit, so that when, for example, a tense situation requires clarity and perhaps a quick decision, you can almost bend time, automatically dip into your "toolbox of stillness," use your best judgment, and take an unapologetic course of action.

When you are taking care of your visual, auditory, physical, and spiritual diets, you are exposing yourself to the stimuli that will help you feel alive. Since you are staying fed, you are avoiding the pitfalls of stagnancy. If we keep ourselves fed with things we enjoy and love, we maintain the momentum required to stay motivated and fulfilled, allowing us to be curious enough to move out of our comfort zones and grow in unexpected ways. And most of all, taking care of ourselves allows us to be more capable of loving others.

A Gift to Myself: My One-Day Retreat

Below is a schedule of what I imagine my personal perfect ordinary day would be. It includes many of the things I value, enjoy, and currently practice—things that help me avoid stagnancy. In the body of the schedule, you will find recipes, reflections, reminders, and rituals.[41] If I were to hold a one-day retreat for myself, this is what it would look like:

6:00-6:30 a.m.	Wake-up
	Wash face
	Brush and floss teeth
	Drink glass of water
	Put on workout clothes
	Pray for 5 min.
	Eat granola or rice bar
6:30-7:30	Write in journal
7:30-7:35	Put on handwraps
7:35-8:00	Drive to gym
8:00-9:00	Muay Thai training

Reflection #1: Not only do I feel awake and alert after training, but I also feel more familiar with my body and what it can do. With practice, my physical capabilities will become locked into my muscle memory, allowing me to readily draw from my physical gifts whenever it's necessary to defend myself. I also look forward to improving my ability to defend my will.

---

[41] This schedule does not reflect one of my typical days. However, it does reflect activities I have spread out across the course of two to three days. Of the activities listed in the schedule, I most regularly practice praying, writing, Muay Thai, preparing the Stickmon Smoothie, and staying in contact with good friends.

As a fairly new student of martial arts, I have learned more about my body and my emotions than I ever expected. These last three years of Muay Thai with Ra'Karma Young, as well as my brief training in the Kamatuuran School of Kali with Gura Michelle Bautista and Balintawak Arnis with Grandmaster Ver Villasin, have taught me that the human body can be lethal. Therefore, it is important to take care of how it is used. Though Muay Thai has been a good outlet for my anger and stress, I've learned quickly that anger cannot be the driving force in an altercation. Explosive, unchannelled anger can lead to unintentional outcomes. Concentration and control are vital. And at the same time, thinking too much can slow me down. Sometimes when I'm training, I find myself becoming too cerebral, too controlled. This is when I realize there is still an imbalance between my intellect and my body.

Reflection #2: The energy boost I get from the workout sustains me throughout the day. The endorphins run through my body, improving my attitude about my life's direction and my ability to accomplish my short-term and long-term goals.[42]

9:00-9:20   Drive home

9:20-9:50   Shower
                 Pick flowers from yard; put one in my hair
                 and put the rest in water

---

[42] "Exercise and Depression," *WebMD*, accessed June 22, 2012, http://www.webmd.com/depression/guide/exercise-depression.

Eat breakfast:

- ➤ 1-2 hard-boiled eggs

    or

- ➤ Greek yogurt with honey, peanuts, chocolate chips (60% cacao), and grapes

and

- ➤ Stickmon's Smoothie:
    - ○ 1 cup raw organic spinach (or kale)
    - ○ ½ cup vanilla soy milk
    - ○ ½ avocado
    - ○ ½ banana
    - ○ ½ cup açai berries, juice or powder
    - ○ handful of strawberries or blueberries
    - ○ ½ cup hibiscus tea
    - ○ 1 tablespoon honey
    - ○ 1 tablespoon flaxseed oil

Pack lunch:

- ○ Egg salad sandwich
- ○ Tuna spread with crackers

o   Blanched asparagus
o   Chips
o   Water
o   Granola bar
o   Trail mix
o   Orange
o   Blueberries
o   Container of raw spinach and pickled beets
o   Cucumbers

9:50-10:10   Meditate

Ritual: Meditate for 20 minutes in morning and evening everyday.[43] (If you can only do 10-15 minutes, that's okay. Do what you can.) Light a candle. Burn your favorite incense (optional). Play meditative music (optional). Take a deep breath and exhale. Do this three times. Close your eyes and sit in a comfortable position you can hold for the allotted time. [My two favorite positions are sitting in a chair (with Lombard support), resting my hands on a pillow on my lap or sitting on two stacked meditation pillows (which rest on a thick blanket), with my knees bent and my feet behind me.] Set the timer. Listen to your breath or repeat a mantra. If any

---

[43] "How Long to Meditate and How Often to Meditate," *The Guided Meditation Site*, accessed June 22, 2012, http://www.the-guided-meditation-site.com/how-long-to-meditate.html.

thoughts or images race through your mind, gently raise them up to the Divine and let them go.[44]

Meditation releases endorphins that are associated with good feeling and having a more positive outlook.[45] Meditation reduces levels of cortisol in the body, a hormone activated by stress.[46] With years of experience, meditation can also thicken portions of the brain associated with sensory stimuli, attention, awareness of sensation, and sensory processing.[47] The research of neuroscientist Sara Lazar shows this increase in cortical thickness and how meditation permanently improves the brain's reception of information, including its reception and awareness of intuitive information.[48]

10:10-10:30   Spend time with/Call/Skype Mom or Dad

Reminder. "Mom" or "Dad" can be anyone you identify as a mother or father figure. Doesn't need to be biological mother or father. Preferably an elder who has been an endless source

---

[44] The Hesed Community in Oakland, CA, part of the World Community for Christian Meditation, had a great influence on my meditation practice. I have incorporated some of what I have learned from that community and tailored those lessons to my own spiritual needs.

[45] "The Benefits of Meditation," *Depression Guide*, accessed June 21, 2012, http://www.depression-guide.com/meditation-benefits.htm.

[46] Elizabeth Scott, "Benefits of Meditation for Stress Management," *About.com*, last modified April 2, 2012, http://stress.about.com/od/tensiontamers/p/profilemeditati.htm.

[47] Lynne McTaggart, *The Intention Experiment: Using Your Thoughts to Change Your Life and the World* (New York: Free Press, 2007), 74.

[48] Ibid., 72-75.

of support and guidance for you. Someone who accepts you no matter what.

10:30-12:30 p.m. Botanic Garden (Tilden Park, Berkeley, CA)

Reminder. Drive to Botanic Garden without listening to music on the way. Once you arrive, allow yourself to walk aimlessly. Don't choose a path; let the path choose you. Let the walk be a prayer. Pay attention to your breath and thank the Divine for it. The trees, plants, and flowers have their own vibration. If you are accustomed to moving quickly in order to be efficient, then pay attention to what it feels like to adjust your pace to the pace of the trees, plants, and flowers. Walk slowly, with the single purpose of noticing and accepting the gift of your surroundings. Pay attention to those trees, plants, and flowers that fascinate you with their beauty. Don't ask why; just be present to them. They may have some answers for you.

11:30-1:30 Pick up close friend and drive to the Armstrong Redwoods

Reminder. The close friend can be your spouse, significant other, best friend, close relative, or spiritual sister/brother/cousin. Whoever it is, make sure it is someone who enjoys nature (or is at least open to the idea) and knows how to be silent.

> Eat lunch in car
> Listen to favorite music

➤ Stickmon's *On the Way*
Playlist:

- o "Dr. Knockboot
  (Instrumental),"
  Nas
- o "Sex, Love, and
  Money
  (Instrumental),"
  Mos Def
- o "Tried by 12
  (Instrumental),"
  East Flatbush
  Project
- o "Passin' Me By,"
  The Pharcyde
- o "Chief Rocka,"
  Lords of the
  Underground
- o "Ain't No Future in
  Yo' Frontin',", MC
  Breed and DFC
- o "Me, Myself & I,"
  De La Soul
- o "Rebirth of Slick
  (Cool Like Dat),"
  Digable Planets
- o "Tha Cipha
  (featuring Rob
  Swift & Roc

Raida)," Triple Threat DJs

- "Step into a World (Rapture's Delight)," KRS-One
- "Double Trouble," The Roots
- "Get By," Talib Kweli
- "The Humpty Dance," Digital Underground
- "So Fresh, So Clean," OutKast
- "The Rain (Supa Dupa Fly)," Missy Elliot
- "Love of My Life (An Ode to Hip Hop)," Common, Erykah Badu
- "You Got Me (featuring Jill Scott)," The Roots, Jill Scott
- "To Zion," Lauren Hill
- "Sobeautiful," Musiq Soulchild

- "Play," Goapele
- "Naughty Girl," Beyoncé
- "Whine Up (featuring Elephant Man)," Kat DeLuna
- "Redemption Song," Bob Marley and the Wailers
- "Dispear," Damian Marley and Nas
- "A Lo Cubano," Orishas
- "Power," Kanye West
- "Home of the Brave," Mr. Lif
- "ElectriK HeaT-the seekwiLL," K-OS
- "No Church in the Wild," Jay Z, Kanye West
- "Loose Wires/Blink Radio," Kenna
- "Green Light (featuring Andre 3000)," John Legend

- o "Things Are Getting Better," N.E.R.D.
- o "Sunday Morning," K-OS
- o "Say Goodbye to Love," Kenna
- o "Enter Galactic (Love Connection, Pt. I)," Kid Cudi
- o "Skeleton Boy," Friendly Fires
- o "Paris (Aeroplane Remix)," Friendly Fires
- o "Constant Surprises," Little Dragon

Reflection: The *On the Way* playlist is a nice, fun balance of the pure and the profane, the ignorant and the introspective. It's as if I brought the hottest club downtown right into my front seat. This playlist gets me amped, and sometimes keeps me chill—either way, it's a source of catharsis, helping me know everything will be just fine. The songs reveal the heart of a relentless fighter and a hopeless romantic who seeks clarity when in battle and when at peace. These songs also remind me that a little bit of braggadocio doesn't hurt in the world of the strong, fit, and the sexy.

1:30-3:00   Walk the trails of the Armstrong Redwoods

Reminder: Like the visit to the Botanic Garden, let the walk be a prayer. Take a deep breath and thank the Divine for it. Allow yourself to wander. Slow down with the trees.   Walk slowly, noticing and accepting all the trees have to offer. Be open to their magic. Know that these trees hear and see everything. They live and have strong spirits. They absorb the stories of the present. What stories, what truths do the trees share with you? What stories would you like to share with the trees?

3:00-5:00   Return home
                   Listen to favorite music
                   ➢ Stickmon's *On the Way Back* Playlist:
                        o "El Fuego Y El Combustible," Jorge Drexler
                        o "This Woman's Work," Maxwell
                        o "Fly Love," Jamie Foxx
                        o "Soledad," Jorge Drexler
                        o "May It Be," Enya
                        o "I Am," Christina Aguilera
                        o "Somebody," Depeche Mode

- o "Thank Heaven 4 You," Esthero
- o "Council of Elrond," Lord of the Rings Soundtrack
- o "Green Forests, Lush Meadows and a Soft Rain Falling," Pure Sounds
- o Listen to nature sounds: ocean waves, rainfall, flowing creek water

Reflection: The *On the Way Back* playlist is mellow. After a meditative walk, it gently ushers me back home. The rhythm and melody of each song bring me to a place my intuition fully understands long before my intellect can get there. It is for this reason I believe that many of these songs are just as magical as the Armstrong Redwoods.

5:00-7:00   Cook and eat dinner
               Lavender Lamb with Quinoa and Broccoli

- o Lamb: season lamb with lavender, salt and pepper; sear both sides; bake for

20-25 minutes at 375°F
- ○ Quinoa: sauté onions, celery, garlic, and shrimp in olive or avocado oil; add chicken broth, quinoa, and oyster sauce; simmer until quinoa is clear
- ○ Blanched broccoli
- ○ Glass of dessert wine
- ○ Red Velvet cupcake

Reminder: While baking lamb, write in your journal. Reflect upon the day. Write whatever comes to mind, emptying your thoughts and feelings onto the page—unfiltered and uncensored.

Secondly, ask yourself, "What do I value?" This question allows you to get reacquainted with yourself. Don't set any goals. Don't place any demands on yourself. Don't attempt to justify your values. Just allow them to surface, and write them down in your journal. Once these values are committed to paper, it can become more natural to make life decisions that are consistent with those values.

7:00-7:25 p.m.   Drive to massage therapist

7:30-8:30 p.m.	Massage
8:40-9:05 p.m.	Return home
9:05-10:30 p.m.	Affirmation ritual

> ➤ Instructions:
>> ○ Make a list of all the things you love about yourself.
>> ○ Write each quality on a 5" x 5" square of your favorite stationery. Fold into tiny squares.

Ritual: Sit in front of a full-length mirror, completely naked. Surround yourself with a circle of candles, flowers, and folded squares of paper. In front of you, create a circle of flowers. Inside the circle of flowers, place a written intention that reads: *May my spirit know love and give love.* Look at yourself in the mirror, and repeat this intention aloud. Massage your face. Massage your hands, your feet, and any other part of your body that has been neglected or overworked.

In your own words, thank the Divine, all the gods and goddesses, and all the ancestors for their guidance and for the wonderful people they have placed in your life. Pray that you will continue to recognize and be open to all the blessings they lay before you.

10:30-6:30	Brush and floss teeth

Wash face
Take daily vitamins (including fish
oil pills)
Drink glass of water
Sleep

Beauty Revealed: Bringing Out the Best in Others

Preface

Exploring what it means to "bring out the best" in others was a collaborative endeavor that began in 2011 between colleague Carlos Hagedorn and I. Reflecting upon how much pain and neglect exists in the world, we believed that based on our experience as educators and our work in the community, we could offer some tools that could perhaps spare people the anguish of being treated in harmful ways. We wrote separate articles about how we as human beings could draw out the best qualities in others. [49] "Beauty Revealed" is my personal reflection on how to achieve this goal. The piece is intended for adults who are interested in: 1) having a positive impact on others, 2) building healthy, meaningful friendships while maintaining good boundaries, and/or 3) deepening bonds with those who mean the most to us.

I am speaking from the perspective of humanities professor with several years of experience teaching high school and college students. I am not speaking from the perspective of a licensed therapist or any other licensed mental health professional; therefore, this article does not cover points outlined by mental health professionals in a letter of informed consent. It is not intended to be an academic paper, nor is it intended for use as a means of seducing others.

---

[49] Both articles can be found at www.bringoutthebest.wordpress.com.

This article is simply intended to be a personal reflection to add to the public discourse regarding how healthy, caring, and civil connections can be made and strengthened.

At the end of this article, you will find a short bibliography because throughout the writing process, I primarily drew from my years of experience working with others as a youth minister and camp counselor and, as mentioned earlier, working as a high school teacher and college professor. Through this experience, I have learned and fine-tuned my behavior in ways that allow me to bring forth the best qualities in other people. I do not profess to be an expert. Instead, I view myself as someone who is in the process of cultivating the very skills that I outline in this article; if I perfect these skills by the time I am 100 years old, I will be very happy.

Secondly, I have drawn from the modeling of others—family, friends, acquaintances, and mentors—who have had a profound impact on my emotional and spiritual well-being. You will find the names of these individuals at the end of this article in a list I call the "Human-Bibliography." One of the main reasons I am capable of writing a piece like this is attributed to the many loving people who have entered my life and brought out the best in me. Citing the lives of real, living human beings and the direct influence they have had on my life seems more relevant, applicable, and compelling since the subject matter involves the *real* ways we can have a positive and fruitful impact on one another.

The thoughts shared in this reflection are offered as suggestions. As with "A Perfect Ordinary Day," you have the freedom to accept, trash, rework, and/or augment these suggestions. Some of what you read may confirm what you already practice. Other ideas may challenge your current lifestyle. You may discover that you have something to add to my recommendations. Whatever the case, I invite you to sit with your response to my article, examine other texts, reflect on your own personal experience, and use your best judgment when deciding what is the most effective means of "bringing out the best" in others.

Introduction

Imagine walking through the world and finding that everything you pass, everything you touch comes to life—wilting plants gradually stand tall; the sick become healthy and full of vitality; weeping children begin to play and laugh; an elderly couple with dulled senses experience the world in all its splendor; abused animals jump and play and resume being partners with humans on Earth; old, abandoned buildings become brand new. In each case, the person, the being, the thing responds to the rejuvenating spirit that lies within you. Consequently, they heal and grow. It's not so much that you plant something new within the living being. The beautiful gifts that already lie within that being are simply recognized, affirmed, and nurtured by you, thereby allowing the person or object the freedom to flourish on their own. The gifts that lie within them are awakened by your presence.

Indeed, "bringing out the best" in others is not as easy as simply walking past people and immediately seeing them come alive. "Bringing out the best" requires the cultivation of a set of qualities and skills. In this endeavor, you may notice the other person experience gradual change, perhaps filled with extreme self-doubt and many mistakes along the way, or you may see quick, continuous, and unwavering transformation. No matter the case, the cumulative effect we will witness will be positive, healthy, and exciting.

So, what does "bringing out the best" in a person mean? Part of it means taking what is dead and bringing it to life. By nature, anything that is alive has the potential to change and grow. When a person's ability to grow is hampered, they are stagnant and see themselves withering away to the point where they feel as though there is no reason to live.

When a person grows, she feels exhilarated and begins to blossom for all to see. Growth begins with a seed: a belief that one is capable of anything. From there, her potential has no bounds. She becomes hopeful and open to the world's possibilities. She decides to learn and take risks all for the purpose of becoming more capable of engaging with the world in healthy, open, and powerful ways. The person accepts the death of old, unproductive prisons of ideas and practices, and embraces a transformation that brings joy and generates life. Essentially, the person's spirit is liberated.

Secondly, "bringing out the best" in someone means accepting and affirming a person for all that he is in the present. This calms an anxious spirit that has been long crippled by criticism and hatred—a criticism and hatred that he may or may not be aware of. Since he is not being tugged or strangled by your will, that person can breathe; the person can freely choose *what* he will transform into and *how* he will transform. When this happens, the person feels like he can be himself—his most authentic self. Self-integrity isn't compromised. And once again, he realizes anything is possible and discovers that he is far more capable of accomplishing the extraordinary than he originally thought.

Clarity of Spirit

If we are committed to "bringing out the best" in all those we encounter, we must first be committed to loving ourselves and steadying our spirits, having a clear sight of who we are in the world. We must possess the conviction that we deserve our freedom, we deserve to be treated justly, and deserve to be loved. We must be committed to caring for ourselves spiritually and physically, and in doing so, make the conscious decision to live. This love and clarity of spirit radiates from us. No one can deny its presence. No one can deny its power. It creates a stir within another human being that inspires that person's best qualities to overflow without warning.

When we love ourselves, stay in tune with our values, and constantly feed our spirits in the name of self-care, we can experience an abundance of joy and become better capable of sharing ourselves with others. As we take care of ourselves, we find that we can't help but listen and sit with a person and explore their thoughts, feelings, needs, longings, worries, and dreams. Hearts are mended by the love that emanates from us.

Human dignity is affirmed when a heart is mended, and the best aspects of one's humanity are drawn out. When we successfully affirm the spirit of another, the person may exhibit many of the qualities below:

honesty
generosity
confidence
optimism
forward-thinking
emotional balance
exuberance

self-fulfillment
self-motivation
ability to take risks[50]
genuine value of self
genuine value of the gifts/skills of others
desire to create
commitment to living
commitment to loving, healthy relationships
commitment to having a
    beneficial impact on one's environment[51]

Being Present

Being present is the foundation for intimacy. In order to be fully present to another, it is important to slow down our pace to give patience room to breathe and develop. Patience enables us to be present to ourselves and to others. When we are patient, we become more open to opportunities for relationship-building and consequently emotional intimacy. Patience is also the building block for other qualities such as persistence, endurance, diligence, and commitment—all of these being various manifestations of "being present." If we do not cultivate a healthy environment for patience to grow in, it can be difficult for these other qualities to develop. If our spirit isn't steady and our pace, our vibration is too fast,

---

[50] Albert Bandura, "Self-efficacy: Toward a Unifying Theory of Behavioral Change," *Psychological Review*, 84, no. 2 (1977): 191-215, http://www.ou.edu/cls/online/lstd5423/pdfs/bandura.pdf.
[51] Albert Bandura, *Self-Efficacy: The Exercise of Control* (New York: W.H. Freeman and Company, 1997), 2-3.

we inhibit the flow of patience and therefore prevent ourselves from being fully present to ourselves and to one another.

Being present to each other doesn't just mean being physically present; however, it can most certainly begin here. The question becomes, "How much of my inner self do I share with the other when I am physically present?" In other words, "How can I become emotionally present?"

To be present in the moment is to be attentive to that moment and all that the moment brings. When we welcome the present moment and its gifts with our complete attention and spirit, emotional intimacy is fed. Our full attention must be offered to the other person during that moment to allow her to feel like she means something to you—to feel like she is valued by you.

There are many things that can potentially interfere with the ability to be present. Below are some examples:

1. Daydreaming: Daydreaming about being with someone else or being somewhere else is not conducive to being in the moment. If your thoughts are frequently fixated on another person or place, this could be an indication of where your true values lie. Therefore, this may be worthy of further self-examination and reflection to know if you need to take a specific course of action and change your commitments.

2. Mechanical devices: Turn off the television. Put the Ipod and Ipad away. Phones need to disappear.

Make a commitment to the real human being you are with and choose not to answer the phone or respond to the text. If the phone rings or if a text comes in, don't be a slave to the device. Answer the phone or respond to the text **later.**

3. Multitasking: Many of us lead extremely busy and demanding lives that may require us to multitask. Just be careful. Constantly assess your priorities and who/what might be competing for your attention. Try to limit or stop multitasking. Even helpful time management tools can have their limits. Some brag about their ability to multitask and in the process fail to recognize how many times they have missed an exit on a freeway or missed an opportunity to affirm their child because their attention was not focused on one thing at a time.

4. Internet usage: One of the many strengths of the Internet is its potential for relationship-building amongst strangers, relatives, and friends. Some, due to circumstances beyond their control, cannot be physically present with another and consequently develop the skill of being emotionally present through email, phone calls, Facebook, etc. Others invest time in developing a strong web presence for business or personal reasons by using some of these tools. If surfing the web, blogging, being on Facebook, or other means of strengthening your web presence compromises your ability to be present to the real

human beings in your midst, then it may be necessary to limit your Internet usage.

Once you have limited or eliminated some of these distractions and are fully attentive, *stay* with the person. *Staying* with a person means not being afraid of the potential for closeness. Allow yourself to be known, but also allow yourself to listen to the person. What is he sharing with you? Does this information give you a sense of what he values in life? Observe the person's facial expressions and body language; scrutinizing the individual or commenting on his every move is unnecessary and may make the person uneasy. Notice the person just enough so that he feels *seen* and not invisible. The most alienating feeling in the world is feeling invisible—as if humanity could care less whether you live or die. To prevent our fellow sisters and brothers from feeling such isolation, share three simple gifts: your presence, your willingness to listen, and your ability to notice the fullness of beauty of the person before you.

Space and Trust

Giving a person space to breathe also "brings out the best" in others. Intimacy is not synonymous with smothering. We can give a person space in a variety of ways. We can give a person physical space—for instance, when you are in his presence, you may keep a comfortable distance between the two of you. This distance may depend on the rapport you have with the person or it may depend on what is appropriate within a given cultural context. Giving space allows freedom for growth—his own personal growth, as well as a growth or a strengthening of the emotional intimacy between you and the other individual.

Space can be given during a conversation as well. As mentioned earlier, listening is an important gift to offer another. Listen to the person's ideas and demonstrate a genuine interest in what the person is sharing. Listen intently for the values that surface and reflect back what you've heard the person share (i.e. "It sounds like you really like _____.") Try not to interrupt. Just wait and listen. Give her story room to wander and be fully expressed. Sit with her and hold her words; don't just let her words slip past you unnoticed. If you are excited about or fascinated with what she has shared or with her way of being, let her know. This can be accomplished by asking questions, sharing a related experience, commenting on how her words reveal a quality about her that you never noticed before, or explicitly saying that she has excited/fascinated/enlightened you with this new information. (i.e. "Wow, I never thought of that before.") Not only can this respect be detected in the words you use, but it can also be detected in the genuineness in your eyes and tone.

When there is space, the conversation has the potential to become a dance—a graceful exchange of ideas and feelings that freely build upon each other. Not competitive or combative. No jousting or using words like ammunition. Just a carefree, fluid dance; both of you will find yourself uplifted by the experience. Trust the direction, the pace, the detour the person takes you in; this demonstrates that you are not trying to control him, but instead this trust allows you to enter his world where your vulnerability is guided by his and vice versa. Have a mutual trust in each other's perspective. And as you enter his world, he enters yours and both of you can enjoy the grace and fluidity of the dance. Through the conversation and being emotionally present to each other, the two of you become willing to take the exchange in an unknown winding direction, exploring the outcome together, indefinitely.

Remember: if you've enjoyed the blessing of being listened to, please don't forget to be a good listener, too—ask the other person about his experience, feelings, thoughts. Be the good listener that he was for you. You don't want your listener to feel invisible.

Throughout the conversation—the dance—make a commitment to keeping the content of the conversation confidential. This helps a person feel safe with you. Don't let what she has shared turn into gossip in the streets! There is a reason why the person trusted you with her story; don't toy with that trust. Recognizing the sacredness of the other and all that she shares is essential. We have the power to either hold or shatter a person's spirit. So, it is imperative to be careful with each others' spirits.

It is important to note that there is a history of people and institutions abusing confidentiality—individuals encouraging or coercing others to keep unjust, dishonest, abusive, oppressive acts confidential because 1) they don't want to experience the consequences of their actions, 2) they are afraid that disclosure of the information will cause a mass frenzy, 3) they don't want to lose the benefits that come with keeping the information quiet, or 4) they fear for their lives.

The only problem is that confidentiality under such circumstances can cause injustice to fester. Injustice likes to disguise itself as innocuous and benevolent; this is one of the many ways it survives and gathers strength and momentum. The best way to deplete injustice of its power is by exposing it and calling it out! One example that prevents the festering of injustice is the role of mandated reporters of child abuse. At the same time, exercise caution.[52] If you suspect the individual is in physical or emotional danger (and may harm themselves or others), encourage the individual to seek the help of a therapist, a suicide hotline, domestic violence shelters, law enforcement etc. Don't try to be a hero and don't try to carry their burden. Under such circumstances, you may also want to seek the advice of a professional to learn the safest and most effective way you can be of help to that individual. For further clarification regarding confidentiality and its limits, please refer to the American Psychological Association's *Ethical Principles of*

---

[52] It is important to first determine if you are a mandated reporter. For a complete list of mandated reporters and related information, please see the websites for the California Department of Social Services and *The Child Welfare and Information Gateway* under the U.S. Department of Health and Human Services. If you are, then legally you are obligated to report the incident to the appropriate authorities and cannot keep that information confidential. If you are not a mandated reporter, please be aware of possible consequences of reporting the incident. For example, the person ("recipient") may deem you untrustworthy and never speak to you again or may claim you misunderstood them. There can be a host of other possibilities; just make sure you understand the consequences of reporting versus not reporting the incident. If you have questions, seek the assistance of a mental health professional or other appropriate authorities.

Psychologists and Code of Conduct.[53]

Control

Honor and respect a person's freedom. The biggest mistake you can make when you meet someone special is to try to possess her forever; all your hopes and dreams are emptied into that single person, often without her consent. Truly the greatest gift one can give a person is the freedom to breathe and the freedom to come and go. Giving a person the mental and physical space away from you (so she is not suffocated by you) helps her to nurture her own needs and desires. As a result, she can be more fully present when the two of you are reunited. It is a manifestation of your love for the individual: that you are secure enough in the friendship and what you have to offer to the friendship; seeing them explore the world without you does not pose a threat. Trying to seize the person and have them all to yourself actually produces the opposite effect: she won't want to be around you at all. Who wants to be around someone who wraps them up in chains?! And besides, why would you want to wrap someone in chains? Pressuring someone to vow her undying allegiance to you (lest you call them a traitor) is not conducive to relationship-building. You don't have an everlasting hold on anyone. Jealously is not proof that you love a person. Attempting to guilt someone into being with you is suffocating. A person should never feel obligated to be

---

[53] "Ethical Principles of Psychologists and Code of Conduct," American Psychological Association, accessed June 28, 2012, http://www.apa.org/ethics/code/index.aspx.

in your presence. She should always be able to breathe, so she can live.

"Bringing out the best" in others should not be used as a means of controlling others. The "recipient" should always have the freedom to accept or reject your support, input, influence, or presence.[54] It is important to acknowledge that the "recipient" has the freedom to not share anything with you. Letting a person know that you support him (and will not berate him) no matter what decision he makes can also give him the freedom to be more open in your presence. This doesn't mean you have to agree with him all the time; sometimes you may have to challenge the person to consider an alternative perspective. Nonetheless, it is still helpful for the "recipient" to know that you will always be a safety net— someone who is there to support him when he take risks; someone who doesn't want him to fall, but will be there to catch him just in case. You need to remind yourself and the "recipient" that he can survive without you. People are free, independent, intelligent human beings who can only grow if their agency is respected.

A desire to control others usually involves some type of fear: fear of being alone; fear that you can't protect your loved ones from harm; fear of how you or the family will be perceived by others; fear that the "recipient" will miss something because he is too slow or too fast; fear that the "recipient" will make the wrong decision. Fear often isn't openly expressed in the form of a statement like, "I am

---

[54] The "recipient" is the person who benefits from your attempts to "bring out the best" in her/him.

afraid." Sometimes it is expressed as anger or sarcasm, or sometimes as silence and isolation. It may also be evident in a person's unwillingness to take risks, and subsequently attempt to project his fears and reservations on others. No matter what form it takes, fear creates massive static in a relationship and interferes with the process of "bringing out the best" in others. Letting go of fears frees up your mind and heart; it gives you a clearer sight of others so you can care for them in ways that allow them to flourish.

Bringing Out the Best—A Dialectic

In the earlier section on space, I spoke of conversation having great potential for becoming a graceful exchange of ideas and feelings—a dance that uplifts the spirits of both people. When dancing, the couple must remain in tune with each other's bodies. When two people interact, both must remain in tune with the comfort level of the other in order for the process to be mutually enriching. The analogy of the dance best captures the nature of all attempts to "bring out the best" in another because of its capacity to create a dialectical relationship. The act of "bringing out the best" in a person can have a transformative impact on both the "recipient" *and* the "giver," and over time can become unconscious and seamless.[55]

In order for the dance to continue, the "recipient" and the "giver" must remain committed to four guidelines related

---

[55] The "giver" is the person attempting to "bring out the best" in the "recipient."

to trust and control:

1. It is important the "giver" does not expect anything in return. Acts that attempt to "bring out the best" in others (consciously or unconsciously) should not operate on a patronage system where favors are exchanged like bargaining chips. For the "giver," the act of giving should be a gift in and of itself because one is practicing the art of being fully human.

2. "Bringing out the best" in others has the potential to inspire the "recipient" to give back to you or to others—not out of obligation, but out of joy and genuine desire. When sharing ourselves, the cycle of receiving and giving has no end. This is also a humble reminder to the "giver" that one should not function as a savior with a Messiah complex; as you are "bringing out the best" in someone (consciously or unconsciously), the other can also be "bringing out the best" in you.

3. Sometimes when a person has grown accustomed to isolation, neglect, and/or mistreatment, the presence of someone who pays attention to the "recipient" can feel extremely powerful and perhaps overwhelming. Some "recipients" may react by pushing you away, while others may become so attached to you that it may cause you to become uncomfortable (i.e. the "recipient" falls in love with you). It is also possible that you may become overwhelming attached to the

"recipient" to the point where you may fall in love with her/him. [56] Under such circumstances, it is important to be clear and honest about your intentions and set necessary boundaries. Use your best judgment in deciding whether this may be: a) a reason to limit your time in each other's presence, b) an opportunity for you to gently refer the "recipient" to a mental health professional, c) explore other options that would ensure the physical and emotional well-being of both you and the "recipient."

4. "Recipients" must graciously receive and be mindful of the amount of heart infused into the action or compliment that has been shared and show gratitude for that gift. As I learned from Evangeline Canonizado Buell, author and community activist in the San Francisco Bay area, "Receiving is also a virtue." For those who have difficulty receiving, saying yes to generosity is a revolutionary act.

Tenderness

Tenderness is a beautiful manifestation of one's emotional center. It is the core of ourselves that loves what's within and knows that that core is intrinsically connected to all within the universe. This inner core is open to being emotionally moved by everything in the universe. It is a touch

---

[56] For more information, research attachment theory, transference, and countertransference.

or a phrase that says, "I see you. I know you exist. You are a gift." When it is genuine and appropriate, expressions of tenderness can be deeply profound.

Tenderness can be found in so many places. It can be found in the soft kisses on the cheek, the temple, the forehead, the lips. It is found when a person embraces another and gently takes in the scent of the beloved. It can be found when the noses or foreheads of two people touch. Tenderness lies in warm hugs and gentle strokes of the back. It is present when you cradle someone in your arms and the person feels like they can surrender. It's quick. It's slow. It can be chaste. It can be romantic. It can be sensual. There are infinite ways of expressing tenderness. Whatever form it takes, being tender has the potential to bring out joy, reaffirm a connection, and/or seal a relationship. Most of all, tenderness helps a person feel loved.

Humility

The wisest people are the ones who have no qualms about publicly admitting when they don't know. The wise women and men I have encountered don't stop at this public admission; they go on to either demonstrate that they are willing to learn and/or thank a person for teaching them something new. This is the epitome of intellectual and spiritual integrity.

Don't try to be a guru. Nobody likes a pompous guru; well, some might if they are addicted to a sycophantic lifestyle. But, usually it's a turn off. Arrogance is the best way to have someone shut the door on you emotionally. Arrogance is a prime indicator of a hidden insecurity. Living your life under the pretense of a know-it-all attitude and then having the public discover exactly how ignorant you are can be quite embarrassing. Being honest about what you know and honest about the limitations of your knowledge leaves an open gap for you to explore meaning with others.

Some also mistakenly confuse humility with self-deprecation. Some may attempt to downplay their strengths because they genuinely fear being viewed as arrogant, while others pretend to be modest in order to mask their true self-absorption. Two of the best reflections that effectively counter such distorted views/practices of humility—reflections that I carry with me to this day—are offered below:

1. An old friend of mine, Glenn Noronha once told me something to the effect of the following: "When you downplay your effect on others, this is not humility; this is just as egotistical as someone who brags about their impact on others. Being humble is about being completely honest about the ways you impact others' lives."

2. When my former spiritual director, Sr. Gloria Loya, P.B.V.M. noticed how often I rejected the compliments she gave me, she stopped and said, "Okay, here's your homework. For every negative thought about yourself that enters your head, I want you to come up with 10 positive things about yourself. And remember, for every time you dismiss

a compliment that someone gives you, you are denying the real impact you had on them. Essentially, you're telling them that their words and their feelings about you mean nothing."

Food

There is nothing like handing a plate of food to someone and witnessing the brightness of their smile. Cooking food for family, friends, acquaintances, and strangers is another reminder that a person is loved and cared for. When you are cooking, it is important to realize that you have the power to infuse love into your food. This can be your love of cooking, love for the people you are cooking for, love for the food itself, and/or love of the ancestors who passed down the recipe to you—those ancestors you know and those ancestors you don't know. The beauty lies in how the "recipient" can taste that love.

Favorites

The first time a friend surprised me with my favorite candy bar, it brought me to tears. I couldn't even remember telling her what my favorite candy bar was. The beauty of the experience was that she paid attention to something I shared in conversation and acted on it—buying that candy bar for me *just because*. We can learn about one another's favorites by explicitly asking, listening to what they happen to share in conversation, or by observing what they consistently gravitate toward in a particular setting (i.e. in a store, in nature, etc.) A person could have a favorite ice cream, food, wine, coffee, flower, animal, song, color, quote, book, actor, sport, movie, scientist, or philosopher. Who knows? Find out and see what happens. Demonstrating that you pay attention to the favorites of another has a way of brightening a person's day, as well as their spirit. It shows that you have allowed your world to be affected by theirs.

Everyday Tips

From maintaining a clear spirit and being fully present to the importance of humility and tenderness, we have explored a full range of approaches to "bringing out the best" in all people we come in contact with. Other quick but essential hints that should also be integrated into our daily endeavor to "bring out the best" in others are listed below:

1. Celebrating Accomplishments: Celebrate in each other's accomplishments. Don't be jealous. Don't tell them they were just lucky. Don't be distracted by your own self-pity and start talking about how you wish good things happened to you. Rejoice in the good things that happen in the lives of others.

2. Showing Gratitude: Express your gratitude in every way possible. This demonstrates that you acknowledge the precious impact others have on your life. Say thank you for everything. You can say thank you face-to-face, via email, Facebook message, text, or a thank you card. If someone touched your

heart—stranger, friend, lover, acquaintance—take the time to let them know how much they mean to you. Life is too short.

3. Acknowledging Names: Know and remember a person's name. Watch a person's body language when you address them by name: their face lights up and their body straightens up or relaxes. They've been acknowledged. It gives the impression that the person is important to you—so important that you remembered their name.

4. Achieving Justice: A quick and simple formula for justice is the following:

JUSTICE = APOLOGY + CHANGE IN BEHAVIOR
+
COMPENSATION FOR LOSSES

This formula is inspired partly by my teaching experience and partly by an article entitled, "Forgiveness: The Last Step," by Marie Fortune who discusses the essential elements for justice within the context of abuse. [57] If you harmed someone intentionally or inadvertently, it is not enough to feel bad about it in the privacy of your bedroom or office. Own your mistakes, your shortcomings, your failures,

---

[57] Carol J. Adams and Marie M. Fortune, *Violence Against Women and Children—A Christian Theological Sourcebook* (New York: Continuum Books, 1995), 201-206.

and redeem yourself using the formula above. And remember, the "recipient" has the freedom to accept or reject your apology (or any other attempts to be redeemed or forgiven). When justice isn't achieved, this can yield skepticism, distrust, and hyper-vigilance amongst the victims. Justice is served by honest communication. Honest communication breeds trust and facilitates the process of "bringing out the best" qualities in others.

Conclusion

Being human is commonly equated with vices and the failings of humanity (i.e. mistakes, hatred, and oppression). Rarely is humanity described in terms of its inherent goodness. Being open to sharing and receiving that goodness is part of what it means to *choose to live* and be fully human. *Choosing to live* and maintaining a clear spirit transforms us into that person who simply walks by and brings all things to life. We see the full range of possibilities for drawing out the best in the world: from knowing a friend's favorite ice cream to remembering a student's name; from telling the bus driver thank you to being a good listener to a coworker; from giving your wife a warm embrace to taking the time to hand a stranger some tissue. Through these simple acts and more, we are *choosing to live*, thereby allowing others to live. When we *choose to live*, our inner beauty emanates from us; this becomes contagious and inspires the beauty that *already* exists in others to grow and blossom. When this great dance takes place, we have not only reached the height of our human potential, but we have also strengthened the umbilical cord to our collective human core—that life-generating source which is good, wholesome, nurturing, and compassionate.

Bibliography

Adams, Carol J. and Fortune, Marie M., *Violence Against Women and Children—A Christian Theological Sourcebook*. New York: Continuum Books, 1995.

Bandura, Albert. *Self-Efficacy: The Exercise of Control*. New York: W.H. Freeman and Company, 1997.

Bandura, Albert. "Self-efficacy: Toward a Unifying Theory of Behavioral Change." *Psychological Review*, 84, no. 2 (1977): 191-215. http://www.ou.edu/cls/online/lstd5423/pdfs/band ura.pdf.

"Child Abuse Mandated Reporter Training California—Who Should Report." California Department of Social Services. Accessed July 16, 2012. http://www.mandatedreporterca.com/who/who.htm .

"Ethical Principles of Psychologists and Code of Conduct." *American Psychological Association*. Accessed June 28, 2012. http://www.apa.org/ethics/code/index.aspx.

"Mandatory Reporters of Child Abuse and Neglect: Summary of State Laws." *Child Welfare Information Gateway*. Accessed July 16, 2012. http://www.childwelfare.gov/systemwide/laws_polic ies/statutes/manda.cfm.

Human-Bibliography

Gerardo Aldana

Anida Yoeu Ali

Fr. Patrick Baraza

Edward Beanes

Lisa Bonta-Sumii

Bill Buell

Evangeline Canonizado Buell

Scott Caballero

Emerita Caballero

Ken Cerreta

Gigi Leung Chow

Janet Cobb

Willie Cobb

James Cones

Cesar Cruz

Lisa Directo-Davis

Jeff Duncan-Andrade

Ibrahim Abdurrahman Farajajé

Diana Ernyei

Fr. Eddie Fernandez

Sharon Gocke

Carlos Hagedorn

Andrew Jolivette

Robert Karimi

Cheryl Kirk-Duggan

Lu Le

Edwin Lozada

Sr. Gloria Loya

Sr. Eva Lumas
Wade Nobles
Glenn Noronha
Mel Orpilla
Fr. Kenan Osborne
Fr. Patrick Philbin
François Pincemin
Alison Rodriguez
Ch'aska Rojas-Böttger
Fermon Stickmon
Lucrecia Mendoza Stickmon
Diana Shepardson
Tom Shepardson
Charles Stickmon
Shawn Taylor
Chief Luisah Teish
Eileene Tejada
Shin Yi Tsai
William Weddington
Dolores Weidemann
Gwen Wilson
Ra'Karma Young

ACKNOWLEDGMENTS

Thank you to all the healers who listened to my thoughts and read my work long before I considered writing this book. Thank you to all the people who asked me, "So how are you?" and genuinely wanted to hear my answer. Thank you to Poonam Whabi of Design Action Collective who once again did a phenomenal job designing the cover. Thank you to the Filipino-American National Historical Society (F.A.N.H.S.) and Philippine-American Writers and Artists, Inc. (P.A.W.A.) for always supporting my work. To P.A.W.A. for sponsoring the book launch party, especially Edwin Lozada for your vision and your attention to detail. Thanks to Mazdak Khamda, Tricia Ong, Cesar Cruz, Michelle Bautista, Angela Efe, and Daria Nile for agreeing to be a part of my book launch party; it has been a pleasure learning about your artistic process and creating with you. Thank you to my Dad, Tom Shepardson and his wife Diana, for always making time to take care of me when I need it the most. Thank you to Mama/Auntie Vangie Buell for having such a big, warm heart and a gentle, fiery tongue; your determination and your ability to listen are an inspiration to me. To my cousin Alison Rodriguez and her husband Martin for being models of generosity. To Mary and John McKey, thank you for all the family dinners and thank you for accompanying Shawn and I on this crazy journey called parenthood. Thank you to Lisa Directo-Davis, Cha'ska Rojas-Böttger, and Anida Yoeu Ali for our coffeeshop and Skype conversations...near or far, you'll always be my sisters. Thank you to Carlos Hagedorn for your integrity and for being a fellow visionary. To Gigi Leung Chow and Nancy Vernes Beltran: It's great to be reunited; your friendship has been priceless. Thank you to Janet and Willie Cobb for sharing nutrition tips and for sharing insights that have always brought so much meaning to the very complex and not so complex things in life. Thank you to Ra'Karma Young for your sense of humor and all that you've taught me in Muay Thai. Love and many thanks to my husband, Shawn Taylor for being a great writer and father; thank you for the MacBook that made writing this book possible; thank you for "feeding" yourself and for learning to grow with me...may the next 10 years be better than the first 10 as we learn even more about each other. To my daughter: you were the inspiration for the title...thank you for being incapable of containing your joy. I love you so much. You've changed me permanently. My utmost gratitude to Jesus, Yemaya, Oshun, Bathala, Diyan Masalanta, Lakapati, Eshu, the ancestors, and my beloved parents, Lucrecia Mendoza Stickmon and Fermon Stickmon for surrounding me with love no matter where I go. Thank you to all the donors and members of the Broken Shackle Publishing family:

Larkin Members

Lance Adderly
Terry Bautista
Athena Bell
Evangeline Canonizado Buell
Cynthia Bonta
Kate Deveney Chilton
Catherine Ceniza Choy
Brenda Crudo
Lorraine Currelley
Cesar Cruz
Carlos Hagedorn
Luciana Huang
Emily Lawsin
Araceli Leyva
Susan Linkhorn
Rebecca Mabanglo-Mayor
Lisa Suguitan Melnick
Angela Muñoz
Wade Nobles
Ch'aska Rojas-Böttger
Luisa Penaranda
Benjamin Pimentel
Lisa Bonta Sumii
Glynda Velasco
William Weddington
Kathy Yee

Gold Taraji Members

Edwin Lozada
François Pincemin
Gwen Wilson

Zulu Spear Status

Michael Cole

BIBLIOGRAPHY

Adams, Carol J. and Fortune, Marie M. *Violence Against Women and Children—A Christian Theological Sourcebook.* New York: Continuum Books, 1995.

Andrews, Matthew M. "(Re)Examining (Multi)Racial Identity: Black-Filipino Multiracials in the San Francisco-Bay Area" in *The Berkeley McNair Research Journal.* Berkeley: Trio, University of California, Berkeley, 2005.

Bandura, Albert. *Self-Efficacy: The Exercise of Control.* New York: W.H. Freeman and Company, 1997.

Bandura, Albert. "Self-efficacy: Toward a Unifying Theory of Behavioral Change." *Psychological Review,* 84, no. 2 (1977): 191-215. http://www.ou.edu/cls/online/lstd5423/pdfs/bandura.pdf.

Bhabha, Homi K. "The Other Question...Homi K Bhabha Reconsiders the Stereotype and Colonial Discourse." *University of Washington.* Accessed March 20, 2012. http://courses.washington.edu/com597j/pdfs/bhabha_the%20o ther%20question.pdf.

Bonner, Lonnice. *Nice Dreads: Hair Care Basics and Inspiration for Colored Girls Who've Considered Locking Their Hair.* New York, Three Rivers Press, 2005.

Daniel, G. Reginald. *More Than Black?: Multiracial Identity and the New Racial Order.* (Philadelphia: Temple University Press, 2002).

Goapele. "Play" in *Break of Dawn.* Oakland: Skyblaze Recordings, 2011. MP3.

Gladwell, Malcolm. *The Tipping Point: How Little Things Can Make a Big Difference.* New York: Little, Brown & Company, 2000.

Guevarra, Jr., Rudy P. "Burritos and *Bagoong*: Mexipinos and Multiethnic Identity in San Diego, California" in *Crossing Lines: Race and Mixed Race Across Geohistorical Divide*, edited by Marc Coronado, Rudy P. Guevarra, Jr., Jeffrey Moniz, and Laura Furlan Szanto, 73-95. Santa Barbara: Multiethnic Student Outreach, University of California, Santa Barbara, 2003.

Jafri, Adeeba. *The Path That Allah Made*. New Delhi: Goodword Books, 2003.

Klein, Ernest. *Klein's Comprehensive Etymological Dictionary of the English Language*. New York: Elsevier Scientific Publishing Company, 1971.

Leksander, Susan. "Psychosynthesis and Multiracial Clients: Diversity and Integration of Multiple Selves." San Francisco: California Institute of Integral Studies, 2007.

Malinsky, Alex. "Avocado Oil Circulates with a Healthy Crowd." *Natural News*. Last modified March 23, 2011. http://www.naturalnews.com/031801_avocado_oil_healthy_fats.html.

McTaggart, Lynne. *The Intention Experiment: Using Your Thoughts to Change Your Life and the World*. New York: Free Press, 2007.

Mbeti, John S. *African Religions and Philosophy*. London: Heinemann Educational Books, 1988.

Nobles, Wade. *Seeking the Sakhu: Foundational Writings for an African Psychology*. Chicago: Third World Press, 2006.

Romo, Rebecca. "Blaxican Identity: An Exploratory Study of Multiracial Blacks/Chicana/os in California." Presentation at the National Association for Chicana and Chicano Studies Annual Conference, San Jose, CA, April 1, 2008.

Scott, Elizabeth. "Benefits of Meditation for Stress Management." *About.com*. Last modified April 2, 2012. http://stress.about.com/od/tensiontamers/p/profilemeditati.htm.

Teish, Luisah. *Jambalaya*. San Francisco: HarperCollins, 1985.

Tortello, Rebecca. "The Fall of a Gentle Giant—The Collapse of Tom Cringle's Cotton Tree." *Jamaica Gleaner*. February 25, 2002. Accessed October 15, 2004. http://www.jamaica-gleaner.com/pages/history/story0020.html.

Wilkerson, Isabel. *The Warmth of Other Sons: The Epic Story of America's Great Migration*. New York: Random House, 2010.

"The Benefits of Meditation." *Depression Guide*. Accessed June 21, 2012. http://www.depression-guide.com/meditation-benefits.htm.

"Child Abuse Mandated Reporter Training California—Who Should Report." California Department of Social Services. Accessed July 16, 2012. http://www.mandatedreporterca.com/who/who.htm.

"Ethical Principles of Psychologists and Code of Conduct." *American Psychological Association*. Accessed June 28, 2012. http://www.apa.org/ethics/code/index.aspx.

"Exercise and Depression." *WebMD*. Accessed June 22, 2012. http://www.webmd.com/depression/guide/exercise-depression.

"How Long to Meditate and How Often to Meditate." *The Guided Meditation Site*. Accessed June 22, 2012. http://www.the-guided-meditation-site.com/how-long-to-meditate.html.

"Mandatory Reporters of Child Abuse and Neglect: Summary of State Laws." *Child Welfare Information Gateway*. Accessed July 16, 2012. http://www.childwelfare.gov/systemwide/laws_policies/statutes/manda.cfm.

Taken. Directed by Pierre Morel. 2008. Los Angeles, CA: 20th Century Fox, 2009. DVD.

"The Power of Du'a." *Shaykh Islam*. Accessed June 28, 2012. http://www.islam786.org/powerofdua.htm#92435509.

ABOUT THE AUTHOR

Prof. Janet C. Mendoza Stickmon, author of *Crushing Soft Rubies*, is a teacher, writer, and performer. Stickmon has taught ethnic studies, social justice, history of Christianity, spoken word and algebra at Salesian High School in Richmond, CA for several years. She is currently a professor of Humanities at Napa Valley College, teaching Filipina/o-American Heritage, American Mind I and II, and Intro to Africana Studies. Prof. Stickmon is the founder and facilitator of Broken Shackle Developmental Training—a program that promotes the use of healing techniques to help reduce the effects of internalized racism. Stickmon's memoir, *Crushing Soft Rubies*, has been used as a course textbook at U.C. Berkeley, San Francisco State University, Santa Rosa Junior College and Gavilan College. She is also a spoken word artist who has performed at several venues across the country. Through her literature and performances, she explores issues of love, motherhood, resilience, ancestral connection, and joy. Stickmon holds a Master's of the Arts Degree in Ethnic Studies from San Francisco State University, a Master's of the Arts Degree in Religion and Society from the Graduate Theological Union in Berkeley, and a Bachelor's of Science Degree in Civil Engineering from the University of California, Irvine. Her work has influenced thousands of adults and adolescents for the last seventeen years.

For workshops, presentations, and products, visit
www.brokenshackle.wordpress.com or email
brokenshacklepublishing@gmail.com.

www.ingramcontent.com/pod-product-compliance
Lightning Source LLC
Chambersburg PA
CBHW032008240626
47153CB00003B/1171